Show Up More Spiritually

A Simple Guide to Strengthening Your Faith and Living It Every Day

Jim Sabellico

ONE

Introduction

If you're anything like me, you've probably gone through seasons where you felt like you were doing everything right. Showing up for work, for your family, for your responsibilities. But somewhere deep down, you knew something was missing.

I've lived that season. I could quote Scripture. I could sit through a sermon. I could say the right things when I needed to. But I wasn't really connected. My relationship with God had become more of a concept than a conversation. I wasn't mad at Him. I just wasn't making space for Him. And when I finally slowed down enough to be honest about it, I realized something that changed everything: I had been showing up everywhere except spiritually.

That realization is what gave birth to this book.

We live in a world that celebrates doing. Work harder. Build faster. Prove your worth. Even in faith, that mindset can sneak in. We start trying to perform for God instead of sitting with Him. We treat prayer like a checklist and worship like a task. But faith was never meant to be something you perform. It was meant to be something you live.

Showing up spiritually isn't about becoming more religious or checking more boxes. It's about learning to live with awareness that God is already here. He's in your stress, in your relationships, in your quiet moments, and even in your mess. It's about inviting Him into the parts of your life you've been trying to manage on your own.

This book is not a theology manual. It's not a devotional full of polished phrases or spiritual sound bites. It's a handbook: simple, practical, and real. Something you can pick up when you're trying to reconnect, when you're confused, or when you just need a reminder that God hasn't gone anywhere. Each chapter is a small window into a piece of faith that often gets overcomplicated. My goal is to make it simple enough to apply and honest enough to matter.

You don't have to read it in order. You can jump to whatever chapter you need most that day—prayer, forgiveness, purpose, or relationships. Think of it like sitting down with a trusted friend who's not afraid to be honest about what faith actually looks like in everyday life.

Faith isn't tidy. It's not always peaceful or predictable. It's full of questions, setbacks, and seasons where God feels silent. But silence doesn't mean absence. It means there's something deeper waiting underneath the noise.

If you've ever wondered why faith feels hard, or why connection with God sometimes fades even when you're trying your best, you're not broken. You're just human. And God knows that. He's not asking you to be flawless. He's asking you to be present.

Showing up spiritually is choosing to keep showing up in prayer, in peace, and in presence, even when it doesn't feel easy or clear. It's about creating a rhythm of honesty with God that turns faith from something you do into something you live.

So that's what this book is about. Not performing. Not pretending. Just learning to bring every part of your life back to the center where it belongs.

Whether you read this cover to cover or a page at a time, I hope it helps you take a deep breath, loosen your grip on control, and remember that God's not waiting for you to get it right. He's just waiting for you to come close.

Let's learn what it really means to show up more spiritually.

TWO

Meet the Trinity

If you've ever heard someone talk about "the Father, the Son, and the Holy Spirit" and thought, *that sounds complicated,* you're not alone. For a lot of people, the idea of the Trinity feels abstract, like something reserved for theologians or people with seminary degrees. It can sound like spiritual math that doesn't add up. How can one God be three people? And what does that even mean for real life?

The Trinity isn't meant to confuse you. It's meant to help you understand that God shows up in every way you could possibly need Him to. He isn't three separate gods; He's one God who reveals Himself in three ways so you can experience the fullness of who He is.

Think about your own life for a second. You're one person, but you play different roles every day. You might be a parent, a friend, and a business owner. Each role brings out a different side of you, but it's still you. You don't stop being a parent when you go to work, and you don't stop being a friend when you come home. You just express your love differently depending on what the moment calls for. That's how God operates.

God the Father is the Creator. He's the mind that imagined everything, the one who dreamed you up before you ever existed. He's the provider, the protector, the one who holds everything together when you feel like everything is falling apart. God the Son, Jesus, is the proof that God didn't want to love you from a distance. He stepped into our world, felt what we feel, faced the same struggles, and made it clear that God isn't detached or unreachable. And the Holy Spirit is God's presence with you right now. He's the quiet voice that nudges you in the right direction, the peace that settles in your chest when nothing around you makes sense, and the strength that rises up when you feel like you've got nothing left to give.

If you've ever had a moment where you sensed something bigger than yourself guiding you, that's the Holy Spirit at work. If you've ever looked back and realized something protected you from a bad choice you almost made, that's the Father's care. And if you've ever felt grace in a moment you didn't deserve it, that's Jesus, reminding you that love always has the final word.

People sometimes ask, "If God is real, why doesn't He just show up?" The answer is that He already did. That's what Jesus was. God didn't send an angel to deliver another list of rules. He came Himself. He walked through our world, ate meals, laughed with friends, and cried real tears. He lived the human experience so we could know He understands it. When you pray, you're not talking to someone who can't relate to your problems. You're talking to a God who's felt heartbreak, betrayal, and exhaustion, and still chose love every time.

When Jesus returned to heaven, He didn't leave us on our own. The Holy Spirit stayed behind as the part of God that keeps walking with us. Some people think of the Spirit as a mysterious force, but it's really the most personal part of God you'll ever know. He's the whisper in your heart that says, "Wait," when you're about to rush ahead, or, "Go," when fear is trying to hold you back. He's the voice that reminds you who you are when you start to forget.

Understanding the Trinity changes how you relate to God. Instead of seeing Him as distant or complicated, you start to recognize that He meets you in different ways for different needs. When you need wisdom, you can talk to the Father who planned your life with purpose. When you need comfort, you can talk to Jesus who understands what it means to feel human. And when you need guidance or peace, you can ask the Holy Spirit to steady your mind and strengthen your heart.

You don't need to use perfect words or sound impressive. God isn't moved by polished prayers. He's moved by honest ones. You can say, "Father, I don't know what to do," or, "Jesus, I feel lost," or, "Spirit, I need peace right now," and He will meet you exactly where you are.

Some people still say, "I can't wrap my head around one God being three." That's okay. Faith isn't about mastering the logic. It's about learning to trust what you can't fully explain. There are plenty of things we believe in without understanding every detail. You don't have to know how electricity works to trust that the lights will turn on when you flip the switch. You don't need to understand the mechanics of gravity to believe the ground will hold you when you step forward. Faith works the same way. You don't have to understand every mystery about God to experience His reality.

When you start to see the Trinity not as a puzzle, but as a picture of perfect love, everything changes. You realize God has been showing up for you all along — as a Father who loves you, as a Savior who understands you, and as a Spirit who walks beside you every step of the way.

So maybe instead of trying to figure God out, just start getting to know Him. Talk to Him throughout your day. Thank Him when things go right. Ask for help when they don't. Listen for the quiet sense of peace that follows when you finally stop trying to do everything alone. That's Him. He's not far away. He's right there.

And that's the beauty of the Trinity. One God. Three ways He keeps showing up for you. Always has. Always will.

THREE

Relationship Over Religion

If you grew up anything like me, Sunday mornings probably looked the same every week. You'd get dressed up, sit quietly in a pew, and wait for that moment when you were finally allowed to leave. Nobody meant any harm by it. That's just how it was. Faith was something you did on a schedule. It was serious, structured, and quiet.

But for a lot of people, that kind of routine planted an idea that's still hard to shake. It taught us that connecting with God meant following a set of rules, dressing the right way, and behaving a certain way. It made holiness feel like something you earned instead of something you were invited into.

Somewhere along the line, we started confusing religion with relationship. Religion says, "Do more. Try harder. Follow the steps." Relationship says, "Come as you are." One tries to impress God. The other just wants to know Him.

The problem is that when we get caught up in religion, we actually start blocking the very blessings we're praying for. We convince ourselves that we have to earn God's favor, and when we mess up, we pull away in shame. We stop praying because we don't feel "worthy." We stop showing up because we think we've disappointed Him. And before long, the relationship that was meant to give us life starts to feel like a burden we can't carry.

That's not what God ever wanted.

If you look at how Jesus lived, He spent very little time around religious rule-keepers. He hung out with people who were messy, misunderstood, and in process. Fishermen. Tax collectors. People who had reputations. People who had doubts. The very ones religion tried to keep out were the ones He invited in.

He didn't ask them to memorize verses or check boxes. He simply said, "Follow Me." That's what relationship looks like. It's not a performance. It's a daily walk. Some days you'll walk close, some days you'll drift, but God never stops showing up.

When you approach faith like a checklist, you end up missing the point. You can attend every service, recite every prayer, and still feel far from God. But the moment you start talking to Him like a friend, something shifts. The walls come down. The pressure disappears. You stop trying to earn His love and start realizing you already have it.

For me, that change took time. I used to think God was keeping score. If I did the right things, He'd bless me. If I messed up, He'd be disappointed. It made my faith feel exhausting. But over time, I started to realize He was never waiting for my perfection. He was waiting for my presence.

That's what makes relationship so different. It's not about pretending. It's about being real. You can tell God when you're angry, confused, or tired of trying. You can admit when you're struggling to believe. He's not threatened by your honesty. In fact, that's where the real connection begins.

When you start to see faith through the lens of relationship, everything changes. Reading Scripture stops being homework and starts feeling like a conversation. Prayer stops being a duty and becomes a lifeline. You stop wondering if you've done enough to deserve a blessing and start realizing that blessings flow more freely when your heart is open to receive them.

That's why religion alone can't bring you peace. Rules without relationship just build walls. But when you walk with God as a Father who loves you, those walls start to crumble. You don't have to be perfect. You don't have to get every detail right. You just have to show up with a willing heart.

So if faith has ever felt cold or rigid to you, start small. Talk to God in your car. Whisper a thank-you before bed. Ask for guidance while you're folding laundry or walking into a meeting. It doesn't have to sound spiritual. It just has to be sincere.

God isn't waiting for you to perform. He's waiting for you to connect.

Because the truth is, the more you try to do faith "the right way," the less room you leave for grace to do its work. But when you drop the act and start treating God like the friend and Father He's always been, that's when the relationship starts to feel alive.

And once you taste that kind of connection, you'll never want to go back to empty ritual again.

FOUR

Hearing the Holy Spirit

When people first hear about the Holy Spirit, they often picture something dramatic. They imagine lightning from the sky, a deep voice echoing through the room, or some kind of movie moment that leaves no room for doubt. The truth is, it usually doesn't look anything like that. Most of the time, it's quiet. Almost ordinary. So gentle that you could miss it if you weren't paying attention.

That's what makes it so powerful.

The Holy Spirit doesn't have to shout because He's not far away. He's right there, living inside you, guiding, prompting, and reminding you of what's true. And the way He speaks isn't always through words. It's through a feeling. A pull. A moment of clarity. A thought that seems to appear from nowhere but lands with perfect timing.

You might have experienced it before without realizing it. The thought that told you to take a different route home. The pause that kept you from saying something you'd regret. The sense that someone was on your mind for a reason, and then you reached out only to find out they really needed it that day. Those aren't coincidences. That's the quiet work of the Spirit.

People miss Him because they expect fireworks. But the Holy Spirit's language is peace. When you start to recognize that, you'll notice He's been speaking all along.

Learning to hear Him isn't about mastering some spiritual skill. It's about becoming more aware. When you slow down long enough to listen, you start to see patterns. You start to connect the dots between what you felt, what you did, and how things turned out. Looking backward helps you see how God's hand was moving even when you didn't notice it in the moment. And once you've seen it enough times in hindsight, you start trusting it more in real time.

The next time you feel that quiet nudge, pay attention. Maybe you don't know why you're supposed to send that text, wait an extra minute before responding, or hold off on a decision. You don't have to understand it right away. Just follow the peace. The more you do, the more you'll see how God weaves those small moments into something bigger.

Think of it like learning to recognize someone's voice in a crowd. At first it's hard to pick out, but the more time you spend with them, the easier it becomes. That's what walking with the Spirit is like. The more you acknowledge Him, the clearer He becomes. It's not about chasing signs or waiting for a dramatic encounter. It's about building relationship through daily awareness.

Some people worry that they'll mistake their own thoughts for God's voice. And yes, that happens. But that's part of the learning process too. The Holy Spirit will never lead you in a direction that contradicts love, truth, or peace. His voice is steady, patient, and consistent. It doesn't demand attention. It invites trust.

I've found that the more I reflect on my life, the more I see moments where the Spirit was guiding me and I didn't even know it. The times I avoided something that would have gone wrong. The people who showed up at exactly the right time. The doors that closed that I later realized needed to close. Looking back builds faith because it reminds you that God's been involved in every chapter, even the messy ones.

Over time, listening becomes second nature. You don't have to strain for it. You just start to notice. The more you notice, the more you respond. And the more you respond, the more you begin to see how everything is connected.

So if you've ever wondered whether God still speaks, the answer is yes. You just have to quiet the noise long enough to hear it.

It might not sound like thunder. It might not stop you in your tracks. But it will feel like peace that doesn't make sense, clarity that shows up when you need it most, and strength that seems to come from somewhere beyond you.

That's the Holy Spirit. And the more you see it, the more you'll see it.

FIVE

_____

Discerning God's Voice

Learning to hear God is one thing. Learning to recognize when it's really Him is another.

We live in a world full of voices. Our own thoughts, our fears, our desires, the opinions of others, and sometimes even the enemy all compete for attention. If you're not careful, they start to blend together until you're not sure which one to trust.

That's where discernment comes in.

Discernment is the practice of slowing down long enough to test what you're hearing. It's not about doubting God. It's about making sure what you follow actually comes from Him.

Jesus said, "My sheep listen to my voice. I know them, and they follow me." That means His voice can be recognized. It carries a sound, a peace, and a consistency that doesn't match the noise around it.

Here's how you start to tell the difference.

God's voice always agrees with His Word. He will never tell you something that contradicts Scripture. The Holy Spirit's job is to remind you of what Jesus already said, not rewrite it. So if what you're hearing pulls you toward pride, division, or compromise, it's not Him.

God's voice also carries peace. Not comfort, but peace. Sometimes He will ask you to do something uncomfortable, but His presence will still feel steady underneath it. The enemy rushes and pressures. God invites and assures.

His voice calls you higher. It leads toward humility, patience, and love. It might correct you, but it never condemns you. It doesn't make you feel worthless. It reminds you who you are.

If you want to learn to recognize His voice, start by paying attention to how it sounds compared to everything else. Fear shouts. Pride argues. Temptation flatters. But God speaks in truth and stillness.

Isaiah 30:21 says, "Whether you turn to the right or to the left, your ears will hear a voice behind you, saying, 'This is the way; walk in it.'" That verse isn't about hearing words from the sky. It's about walking closely enough with God that His guidance becomes familiar.

Discernment doesn't come from perfection. It comes from proximity. The more time you spend with Him, the easier it becomes to know what sounds like Him and what doesn't.

And even then, God designed us to confirm things in community. If you believe He's speaking something big, test it. Bring it to Scripture. Pray over it. Ask a trusted spiritual mentor to weigh in. Real guidance will hold up under that kind of light.

The enemy used Scripture to tempt Jesus in the wilderness, twisting truth just enough to sound convincing. Jesus didn't argue. He answered with more truth. That's discernment — knowing the Word so well that counterfeits can't stick.

God's voice won't flatter your ego or feed your fear. It won't demand impulsive action or isolate you from wise counsel. It will point you toward peace, humility, and love every single time.

The more you listen, the more you'll notice how steady it sounds. He doesn't play guessing games. He's not trying to confuse you. He wants you to know Him, and that includes knowing His voice.

So when you're unsure, slow down. Take a breath. Test what you're hearing. Ask yourself: Does this align with Scripture?

Does this bring peace or panic? Does this make me more like Jesus or more focused on myself?

When you can answer those questions honestly, you'll know which voice to follow.

And every time you choose the one that leads you closer to God, your discernment grows stronger.

That's how you learn to hear Him with confidence. Not by forcing it, but by walking closely enough that His voice becomes the most familiar one in the room.

SIX

Understanding Your Enemy

You can't live a life of faith without learning how to recognize what tries to destroy it.

The Bible says we have an enemy, but not the kind most people imagine. He doesn't show up with horns or a pitchfork. He's not hiding under your bed waiting to scare you. He's much more subtle than that.

His name is Satan. And before he was the adversary, he was an angel.

Scripture tells us he was created by God, not as evil, but as good. He was beautiful, intelligent, and gifted with influence. But pride turned his gifts into rebellion. He wanted to be worshiped instead of worshiping. He wanted control instead of surrender.

That's what got him cast out of heaven. Not because God was threatened, but because pride can't exist in the presence of perfect holiness.

It's important to understand this.

Satan isn't God's opposite.

He's not an equal force on the other side of a cosmic chessboard. He's created, limited, and already defeated.

But for now, he's still active. Not all-powerful, not everywhere at once, but persistent. His goal is simple: to distort whatever God designed for good.

That's why the enemy doesn't always attack directly. He deceives.

His greatest trick has never been obvious evil. It's subtle distortion.

He's the voice that whispers, "Did God really say that?" He's the one who tries to convince you that you're too far gone or too unworthy to be loved. He tempts you with shortcuts that seem easier than obedience. He twists truth just enough to make it sound convincing.

He doesn't need to turn you into a villain. He just needs to keep you distracted, divided, or doubting long enough to stop you from walking in the light.

That's how he operates. Always has. Always will.

In Genesis, he used words to make Adam and Eve question what God had already made clear. In the wilderness, he used Scripture itself to try to manipulate Jesus. In both cases, his weapon was confusion.

That's why clarity is one of your greatest defenses. The more you know the truth, the easier it is to recognize what's false.

You don't fight the enemy by yelling at him. You fight by standing firm in truth.

Ephesians 6 says to "put on the full armor of God" truth, righteousness, peace, faith, salvation, and the Word of God. That armor isn't about fear. It's about readiness. You wear it so you can stay steady when lies try to shake you.

James 4:7 gives the whole strategy in one line: "Submit yourselves, then, to God. Resist the devil, and he will flee from you."

Notice what comes first. Submission, not resistance. The more surrendered you are to God, the less power the enemy has over you.

When you walk in light, darkness can't follow.

That's because darkness doesn't exist on its own. It's just the absence of light. Evil is the absence of truth, and the enemy thrives where people live disconnected from it.

But when you live in truth, when you stay close to God, when you recognize your identity in Christ, there's nothing the enemy can take from you.

He can't steal what's been sealed by God. He can't win a battle that's already been decided.

Your job isn't to fear him. It's to stay alert and aware, knowing that you already carry authority over him through Jesus.

Don't get obsessed with studying evil. Get confident in knowing truth. You don't fight darkness by staring into it. You fight it by keeping your eyes on the light.

Because no matter what the enemy throws at you, light always wins.

SEVEN

Divine Design

One of the biggest mistakes people make in faith is thinking they're supposed to figure everything out. Who they are. What their purpose is. Why they're here. We treat it like a puzzle to solve, as if God is waiting with a grading sheet to see if we get the right answer. But that's not how it works. You weren't designed to *solve* your identity. You were designed to *live* it.

When God created you, He wasn't making a prototype. He was crafting something intentional and complete. Every part of you — your gifts, your quirks, your instincts, even your struggles — was formed on purpose. That doesn't mean you'll always understand it, but it does mean there's meaning woven into every thread of who you are. The problem is, most of us spend our lives trying to become what we think we're supposed to be instead of learning how to become more fully ourselves.

It's easy to get caught up in comparison. We see someone else's path, their calling, their confidence, and we start wondering if maybe we missed ours. We chase roles, titles, and validation, hoping that somewhere along the way we'll stumble into the version of ourselves that finally feels "enough." But the truth is, you don't find your worth by achieving more. You find it by recognizing what's already been placed inside you.

Discovering who God says you are isn't a one-time revelation. It's a journey that unfolds over your entire life. At first, the growth can feel fast. You go from not really understanding who you are to suddenly realizing that God has been speaking your identity over you the whole time. It's like seeing the world in color for the first time — things you used to overlook start making sense. You see how your strengths, your story, even your scars, all connect in ways you never noticed before.

But after that initial clarity, something shifts. The pace slows down. You reach a point where it's not about learning new information anymore. It's about deepening your understanding of what's already true. That's the part that takes a lifetime. Like a reverse hockey stick chart, the first 90 percent of the journey happens quickly, and the last 10 percent stretches across the rest of your days. That's not failure. That's design. God set it up that way so you would keep seeking Him, not just the answers.

Because the moment you believe you've "figured it out," you stop listening. You stop growing. And the relationship that's meant to stay alive and evolving becomes something static and stale. God doesn't want you to master Him. He wants you to walk with Him.

Identity in Christ isn't a label you memorize. It's a living awareness that deepens with time. Some days you'll feel strong and sure of who you are. Other days you'll feel uncertain, pulled in every direction, questioning whether you've lost the plot entirely. Those moments don't mean you're failing. They mean you're human. Faith isn't about perfect confidence. It's about constant connection.

If you've ever felt frustrated that you don't "know" your purpose, take a breath. You're not behind. You're actually right where you're supposed to be. God doesn't reveal everything at once because He's not trying to give you a plan to execute. He's inviting you into a relationship to trust.

Think of it like driving with headlights on a dark road. You can't see the whole journey at once, just the next few feet in front of you. But as you move forward, the path keeps revealing itself. That's how divine design works. God gives you enough to take the next step, and with every step, you start to see a little more.

If you look back, you'll probably notice that you've already changed more than you realize. The things you used to chase don't hold the same weight anymore. The fears that used to define you don't hit as hard. The way you make decisions, the way you handle conflict, the way you love people — it's all evolving. That's what growth looks like. Not a finish line, but a steady unfolding.

So maybe instead of trying to "figure out" who you are, you could start practicing *being* who you are. Notice what brings peace instead of pressure. Notice what stirs joy instead of comparison. Pay attention to the quiet convictions that won't go away. That's where God usually speaks identity the loudest — not in the noise of trying to become something, but in the peace of learning to rest in what He's already made you to be.

You don't have to have it all mapped out. You don't have to know the full picture. You just have to keep seeking, keep trusting, and keep becoming. That's the divine design at work. You're not running out of time. You're right on schedule.

EIGHT

Grace Over Guilt

Most people believe in grace as an idea, but live like it doesn't apply to them. They nod their heads when they hear about forgiveness, but deep down they still feel like they owe God something. Like they have to make up for every mistake before they can really move forward.

That's what guilt does. It keeps you living in the past, replaying moments you can't change and trying to earn your way back into favor. It sounds holy on the surface, but underneath it's still about control. Guilt says, "If I try harder, maybe I can make this right." Grace says, "It's already been made right."

The tension between the two is where most people get stuck. We want to believe God has forgiven us, but we still carry the weight just in case. We treat grace like a safety net instead of the foundation we actually stand on.

When you start to understand divine design, you realize guilt doesn't fit into it. God didn't build you to walk around afraid of messing up. He built you to grow. To learn. To keep getting closer. Grace isn't a free pass to do whatever you want. It's the freedom to live without shame while you keep becoming who you're meant to be.

If you've ever tried to live perfectly and failed — which, by the way, is everyone — you know the cycle. You start strong, fall short, feel guilty, then promise to "do better next time." For a while it looks like progress, but it's really just pressure. You're still trying to earn what God already gave you.

Jesus didn't die so you could spend your life stuck in self-punishment. He came to lift that weight off you. Grace doesn't ignore what you did wrong; it transforms how you move forward. It turns shame into strength, and regret into wisdom. It's what allows you to learn from your past without being defined by it.

Think about it like this: guilt is a treadmill, and grace is an open road. Guilt keeps you running in circles, exhausted and frustrated, never feeling like you've gone far enough. Grace takes you somewhere. It invites you to move forward knowing that each step, even the messy ones, is covered.

When you live under guilt, you'll always feel like you're disqualified from closeness with God. You'll stop praying when you need to the most. You'll pull back from people because you don't feel "good enough." But when you start to live under grace, you realize God never asked you to earn His love. He asked you to receive it.

That shift changes everything. Suddenly prayer stops being an apology tour and starts being a conversation. Worship stops being a way to prove devotion and becomes a way to express gratitude. You stop asking, "How can I make this right?" and start asking, "What do You want to show me through this?"

Grace doesn't erase responsibility. It just removes condemnation. It allows growth without fear. That's what makes it so powerful — it fuels transformation without shame as the engine.

There will still be days you fall short, speak too soon, lose your patience, or repeat a pattern you swore you were done with. Grace doesn't pretend those moments don't exist. It just meets you there with love that says, "Let's try again."

The world teaches you to measure progress by perfection. God measures it by direction. As long as you're moving toward Him, you're doing it right.

So maybe it's time to stop apologizing for who you used to be and start thanking God for who He's helping you become. Guilt keeps you trapped in yesterday. Grace gives you permission to live today.

When you really start to believe that, you'll feel lighter. Not because you've done less wrong, but because you've finally realized that grace was never about what you do — it's about what He already did.

And once you grasp that, guilt loses its grip for good.

NINE

Learning to Trust Again

Trust sounds simple until you've had it broken.

Most people don't struggle to believe that God exists. They struggle to believe they can depend on Him. Especially when life hasn't gone the way they hoped, or when people who claimed to represent Him did more harm than good.

If that's you, I understand. It's hard to give your heart to a God you don't fully trust. It's even harder when your history keeps reminding you how that felt last time.

For a lot of us, our trust didn't just break in one big moment. It was chipped away — by disappointment, betrayal, unanswered prayers, or long seasons where we felt forgotten.

Somewhere along the line, we learned that staying guarded felt safer than being open.

The problem is, guarded hearts can't receive what they're protecting themselves from.

When you hold on to control out of fear of being hurt again, you don't stop pain — you stop healing.

But God's not mad at you for being cautious. He's patient. He knows why you're hesitant, and He's not asking for instant confidence. He's asking for willingness.

Trust doesn't start with big leaps. It starts with small yeses.

When you pray again after a long silence, that's trust. When you forgive someone even though you're still hurting, that's trust. When you give God the parts of your story you don't understand, that's trust.

You don't rebuild it all at once. You rebuild it one moment at a time.

Proverbs 3:5 says, "Trust in the Lord with all your heart and lean not on your own understanding." That's not a demand for blind faith. It's an invitation to rest from carrying what only God can handle.

Psalm 27:10 says, "Even if my father and mother abandon me, the Lord will hold me close." That means no matter who walked away, He didn't. God doesn't betray, manipulate, or disappear. He stays.

But I know it's not easy to trust someone you can't see. Especially when you've been hurt by people who claimed to speak for Him. That kind of pain runs deep. It can make you feel like faith itself is unsafe.

If that's you, take this as permission to untangle the difference between **God** and the people who failed you.

The church might have disappointed you. A believer might have betrayed you. But God is not the same as the ones who misrepresented Him.

When you start separating who *He* is from what *they* did, healing begins.

God's version of trust doesn't mean closing your eyes and hoping for the best. It means learning to rest in His character, not your circumstances.

That's what happened with Job. He lost everything — family, health, stability — and still said, "Though He slay me, yet will I trust Him." That's not blind faith. That's deep trust built through pain. Job didn't understand the plan, but he knew God's heart was still good.

You can know that too.

Learning to trust again means letting God show you that He's not like the ones who hurt you. It means giving Him the chance to prove Himself faithful, not because He owes you proof, but because He loves showing you who He is.

The Bible doesn't say you'll always understand what God is doing. It just promises He'll never leave you while He's doing it.

Trust is built in time and tested in storms. The more you bring your fears and questions to Him instead of running from Him, the safer He'll start to feel.

You'll see His consistency. His gentleness. His patience.

And little by little, your walls will lower — not because you forced them to, but because love made them unnecessary.

That's how trust grows. Not by pretending you're fearless, but by walking with God while you're still unsure.

He doesn't need your perfection. He just wants your permission.

Trust begins again the moment you say, "God, I'm scared, but I'm still here."

And that's enough.

TEN

How to Pray

For a lot of people, prayer feels complicated. We worry about saying the right words, using the right tone, or knowing the right moment to start. We treat it like there's a secret code that only certain people know — as if God has a preferred language or a level of formality we have to meet before He'll listen. But that's not prayer. That's performance.

Prayer was never meant to be stressful. It was meant to be conversation. The whole point isn't to impress God, it's to include Him.

Somewhere along the way, people started approaching prayer like they were speaking to a boss instead of a Father. They started editing themselves. They filtered out the frustration, the confusion, and the honesty that makes real communication meaningful. They made it polite instead of personal.

But the truth is, God already knows what you're thinking. He knows when you're angry, when you're disappointed, when you're scared, and when you're just tired of pretending everything's fine. Prayer isn't about informing Him. It's about inviting Him into those moments.

If you've ever hesitated to pray because you thought you'd "do it wrong," remember this: there is no wrong way to talk to someone who loves you. There are no magic words, no perfect tone, no required phrases. Just honesty.

When Jesus taught His disciples how to pray, He didn't give them a speech. He gave them a pattern. He said to start by recognizing who God is, to bring your needs before Him, to ask for forgiveness, and to extend it to others. That's it. Simple. But somewhere along the way, people turned that simplicity into ceremony.

We started treating prayer like a formula instead of a conversation. And that mindset does something dangerous — it sets us up for disappointment. Because when prayer feels like a transaction, we expect immediate results. We ask for something and wait for it to happen, and when it doesn't, we assume it "didn't work."

Prayer isn't a vending machine. It's a relationship. The goal isn't to get something, it's to *stay connected*. Sometimes God answers right away. Sometimes He waits. Sometimes He redirects entirely. But every single time, He responds in a way that protects your purpose and your growth.

If you're only measuring the success of prayer by whether you got what you asked for, you'll miss how often prayer is working in ways you can't see yet. Prayer doesn't just change situations. It changes *you*.

Think about it this way: when a child comes to a parent asking for something, the parent doesn't always say yes, but they always listen. The conversation itself builds trust. That's what prayer does. It builds the connection that keeps your heart aligned with God's even when life doesn't make sense.

Some of the most meaningful prayers you'll ever pray will be the simplest ones. "Help me." "Thank You." "I'm sorry." "Please show me what to do." Those few words hold more power than a thousand carefully chosen ones because they're honest. They come from the heart, not the habit.

You don't need a quiet room or a perfect mood. You can pray while you're driving, washing dishes, sitting in a meeting, or waiting in line. Prayer isn't confined to sacred spaces. Every space becomes sacred when you invite God into it.

And don't be afraid of silence, either. Prayer isn't just about talking. It's about listening. Sometimes the most powerful moments happen when you say nothing at all. When you just sit in the stillness and let God speak in ways that don't sound like words.

The more you do it, the more natural it becomes. And the more natural it becomes, the more it shifts from something you "have to do" into something you can't go without.

So how do you pray? You just start. Be real. Be honest. Be present. Talk like you would to a trusted friend — because that's exactly what He wants to be.

Don't overthink it. Don't wait for perfect conditions. Don't expect fireworks. Just talk. And trust that every word, every sigh, every moment you open your heart, God hears it all.

That's prayer. Simple. Human. Holy.

ELEVEN

Reading the Word With Purpose

If you're honest, the Bible can feel overwhelming. Thousands of pages, strange names, and stories that sometimes don't seem to connect. You start at Genesis with good intentions, make it a few books in, and suddenly you're stuck wondering what any of it has to do with your life today.

You're not alone in that. Most people don't struggle with believing the Bible is important — they struggle with knowing what to do with it.

We've turned reading Scripture into something people feel like they're supposed to *check off* instead of something they can actually *engage with*. We read it when we're desperate, flip through it when we're lost, or search for a verse we can post that sounds encouraging. But the Bible was never meant to be a library of inspirational quotes. It's a conversation. It's God's voice on paper, and every time you open it, He's speaking.

Reading the Word with purpose starts with shifting your mindset. The goal isn't to get through it. The goal is to let it get through to you.

If you only open the Bible looking for something to make you feel better, you'll miss the parts that are meant to make you *different*. God doesn't use Scripture to flatter you. He uses it to form you. Sometimes it comforts, sometimes it corrects, and sometimes it simply reminds you that you're not alone in what you're walking through.

You'll start to notice that when you approach the Word with openness instead of obligation, it comes alive. Verses you've read a hundred times will suddenly hit differently because your season has changed. Something you skimmed last year will meet you right where you are today. That's not coincidence. That's the Spirit making it personal.

It's okay if you don't understand everything you read. Nobody does. You're not supposed to walk away from every chapter with full comprehension. You're supposed to walk away with curiosity. Let the questions lead you deeper instead of making you feel disqualified.

One of the best ways to start is small and consistent. Pick one book — maybe John if you're new to it — and read a few verses a day. Before you start, pause and simply ask, "God, show me what You want me to see." That small moment of invitation turns information into revelation. You're not reading to collect knowledge. You're reading to hear His heart.

And don't rush. Let the words breathe. When something catches your attention, stop and sit with it. Ask yourself why. What is this revealing about who God is? What does it show me about myself? What does it invite me to do differently? That's how Scripture becomes alive — when you stop reading it like a book and start letting it read you.

You'll notice that over time, your responses start to change. You'll have more peace in your decisions, more patience in your reactions, and more clarity in your purpose. That's not magic. That's alignment. God's words start shaping your words. His perspective starts influencing yours.

And when you share verses or insights with others, it'll come from a place of experience, not performance. You won't post Scripture just because it sounds nice. You'll share it because it spoke something real into your life. That's what makes it powerful — not the verse itself, but the transformation behind it.

The Bible isn't a tool to prove your faith. It's the foundation that builds it. You don't need to read it perfectly. You just need to keep showing up to it.

There will be days it feels like a lifeline, and days it feels dry. Keep showing up anyway. Because the more you do, the more you start to recognize a pattern — the same God who spoke in those pages thousands of years ago is still speaking through them now. And the more you read, the clearer His voice becomes.

So don't just read the Word for inspiration. Read it for transformation. Let it stretch you, challenge you, and remind you who you are and whose you are.

Because once you learn to read the Bible not as a rulebook, but as a relationship, it stops being something you have to do and becomes something you can't imagine living without.

TWELVE

Worship as a Way of Life

When most people hear the word "worship," they think of music. They picture a stage, lights, raised hands, and someone singing their heart out. And yes, that can be worship. But it's only one piece of a much bigger picture.

Worship isn't about a song. It's about a spirit. It's the attitude you carry, the way you live, and the posture of your heart toward God.

If music was taken away, you could still worship. If church buildings disappeared, you could still worship. Because worship was never meant to be confined to a room. It was meant to shape how you move through life.

At its core, worship simply means "to give worth." It's whatever you give your best attention, energy, and affection to. Everyone worships something. For some, it's success. For others, it's approval, comfort, or control. Worship is less about what you sing and more about what you *center*.

When you start living with awareness of that, you realize how easy it is to let other things take the place that belongs to God. That's why worship matters — not because God needs constant compliments, but because you need constant clarity. Worship keeps your heart aligned. It keeps your focus steady. It reminds you who's really in control and who's not.

True worship happens in ordinary moments. It's the gratitude you whisper while folding laundry. It's the patience you show when you'd rather snap. It's choosing integrity when nobody's watching. It's doing your work with excellence because you see it as a way to honor God, not just earn a paycheck.

You don't need a microphone to worship. You just need awareness.

When you start seeing worship as a way of life, you stop dividing your world into "spiritual" and "everyday." You realize it's all connected. The same God who meets you in church meets you in the carpool line, the office, the grocery store, and the middle of your chaos.

That shift changes how you carry yourself. You stop chasing perfection and start chasing presence. You start to notice beauty in places you used to overlook. You start to find peace in routines that once felt empty. Because once you begin to see every moment as an opportunity to honor God, life stops feeling divided.

Worship also changes how you see other people. When your heart stays connected to God, you begin to reflect Him more naturally. Your words soften. Your patience grows. Your compassion deepens. You don't have to announce that you're a believer. People can tell by the way you treat them.

Some days, worship will come easy. Gratitude will pour out without effort. Other days, it will feel like a choice you have to fight for. Those are the days it means the most. Because worship isn't about what you feel — it's about what you decide. It's an act of trust that says, "Even if everything around me is uncertain, God, I still believe You're worthy."

When you begin to live that way, the songs you sing start to mean more. They're no longer the moment of connection — they're the overflow of a life already connected.

That's what worship really is: a lifestyle of gratitude and alignment. It's not something you turn on when the music starts and off when it ends. It's the thread that runs through your day, holding everything together with purpose and peace.

So don't limit worship to a playlist or a service. Let it be the way you show up in every part of your life — in your work, your relationships, your decisions, and your attitude.

Because the truth is, how you live *is* what you worship.

THIRTEEN

Hearing God in the Quiet

Most of us live surrounded by noise. Not just the kind that comes from traffic, phones, or conversations, but the kind that comes from our own thoughts. The constant hum of things to do, problems to solve, and worries that won't settle. We get so used to the noise that silence starts to feel uncomfortable.

But that's often where God speaks the loudest - in the quiet.

People sometimes imagine hearing from God as this dramatic experience, like a movie moment where the clouds part and a deep voice fills the room. But in reality, His voice usually sounds like peace. It's subtle. Steady. Gentle. Easy to miss if you're only listening for something spectacular.

God rarely interrupts. He invites.

The challenge is that we've built lives that make it almost impossible to notice. We fill every moment with movement, and when we finally stop, we reach for a distraction to fill the stillness. But the quiet is where connection happens. The quiet is where you start to notice what's really going on in your heart — the things you've been avoiding, the feelings you've been numbing, the prayers you've been rushing through without meaning to.

When you slow down long enough to sit in that space, something sacred happens. You start to realize God was never far away. You just couldn't hear Him over the noise.

Silence has a way of clearing the static. It lets you recognize the difference between anxiety and awareness. Between impulse and intuition. Between your thoughts and His guidance.

At first, it's uncomfortable. You'll notice the temptation to reach for your phone or to fill the quiet with background music. But if you can push past that discomfort, you'll find something deeper waiting. You'll start to feel peace that doesn't make sense, calm that you didn't create, and a sense of direction that feels like it's rising up from somewhere beyond you.

That's how God speaks. Not with chaos, but with clarity.

If you want to hear Him more clearly, start creating more space. It doesn't have to be long or complicated. It could be five quiet minutes before the rest of the house wakes up. A walk without headphones. Sitting in your car before you go inside. You don't have to fill the silence with words. Just be still.

You don't have to force it or chase some big spiritual moment. Just sit, breathe, and invite God into it. You might not "hear" anything right away. That's okay. The goal isn't to produce results. It's to create room.

Because the more space you make for stillness, the more you start to recognize His voice in motion too. You'll notice how peace shows up in your day when you take the time to slow down. You'll see how clarity finds you when you stop trying to figure everything out on your own.

Learning to hear God in the quiet isn't just about solitude. It's about awareness. It's learning to recognize that His presence isn't limited to quiet places. Once you practice stillness, you start to carry it with you. You can be calm in the middle of chaos because you've learned how to tune your heart to His voice no matter what's happening around you.

It's not easy. The world rewards hurry, not stillness. But the spiritual life grows in the opposite direction. Growth doesn't always come from doing more. It often comes from creating space for God to do what only He can do.

So maybe start small. Set your phone down. Sit in the quiet. Let your mind wander if it needs to. Let your thoughts settle when they're ready. And when the noise starts to fade, you'll notice it. That quiet sense of peace that doesn't need words to make itself known.

That's Him. Always speaking. Always near. Just waiting for you to slow down long enough to listen.

FOURTEEN

Finding God in the Everyday

If you've ever wished God would just show up and make Himself obvious, you're not alone. Most people want that moment — the clear sign, the unmistakable voice, the confirmation that feels undeniable. We want to *see* God move. The funny thing is, He's moving all the time. We just don't always recognize it.

Finding God in the everyday isn't about learning to summon His presence. It's about learning to notice what's already there.

We tend to think of spiritual moments as the big ones. The breakthroughs. The healings. The worship nights where you feel something powerful. But the truth is, God often hides His presence in the ordinary. He shows up in the laughter of your kids, in the warmth of a sunrise, in the conversation that happens at just the right time. He's in the small mercies you barely notice — the near-misses, the timely texts, the sudden peace when anxiety should be winning.

You don't need lightning in the sky to know God is near. You just need eyes that are willing to see Him where He already is.

When you start looking for Him in your daily life, everything starts to change. Mornings don't feel as rushed. Work feels less like a grind. Even challenges start to carry meaning because you can sense God shaping you through them. The same drive to work becomes a moment to pray. The same errands become opportunities to show kindness. The same routines that used to feel meaningless become places of worship.

That's the thing about faith — it doesn't remove the ordinary, it redeems it. It takes the same day everyone else is living and gives it a different depth.

Some people think finding God means escaping real life, but it's actually the opposite. It's about learning to meet Him right in the middle of it. He's not waiting for you to get to church or to check off your devotional. He's sitting in the quiet of your morning coffee. He's standing in the middle of your hardest moments, steady and present, even when you don't feel it.

And the more you notice Him, the more you start to see a pattern. The same God who feels close on your best days is still right there on your worst. The same grace that carried you through a storm shows up again in the calm. Over time, you start to realize that connection with God was never meant to come and go. It was meant to be constant.

You don't need to do anything dramatic to find Him. You just have to pay attention. Slow down enough to notice beauty. Be kind when nobody's watching. Speak honestly. Forgive quickly. Let gratitude interrupt your routine. Those are the places where the presence of God becomes real — not because you earned it, but because He's always been there waiting for you to see it.

Once you start finding God in the small things, the big things stop feeling so overwhelming. You start to recognize that even when life feels uncertain, He's still steady. Even when you don't see a way forward, He's still guiding. And when you look back, you'll see His fingerprints all over your story.

That's what it means to find God in the everyday — to stop separating sacred from simple, to stop waiting for some grand encounter, and to start realizing that every breath, every step, every moment can be holy if you let it be.

He's not hiding. He's just waiting for you to look up.

FIFTEEN

Turning the Other Cheek

"Turn the other cheek." You've heard that phrase before, probably so many times that it's lost its edge. Most people take it to mean you're supposed to stay quiet, let people walk all over you, and just keep smiling through it. But that's not what Jesus meant at all.

Turning the other cheek wasn't about being soft. It was about being strong in a different way. It was about power under control.

In the culture where Jesus said those words, a slap on the cheek wasn't just physical — it was social. It was a way of saying, "You're beneath me." It was an insult meant to humiliate. And when Jesus said to turn the other cheek, He wasn't telling people to accept abuse. He was telling them to stand tall. To look that person in the eye. To say, without words, "You don't get to define my worth."

That's not weakness. That's strength rooted in identity.

It's the same kind of boldness that says, "If you've got something to say, say it to my face." Not in aggression, but in calm confidence. It's what happens when you know who you are and whose you are. You don't need to fight to prove your value, but you're also not going to bow to someone else's attempt to take it.

When you really understand what Jesus was teaching, it flips the whole thing around. He wasn't telling people to be doormats. He was teaching them to disarm hate without mirroring it. To hold their dignity without losing their peace. To refuse to play the same game as the people who thrive on conflict and control.

That's hard to do in real life. When someone attacks you, especially unfairly, every instinct in you wants to hit back. Maybe not physically, but with words, with attitude, with silence that cuts deeper than anything you could say. The problem is, when you do that, you lose your center. You hand over your peace to someone who didn't earn it.

Turning the other cheek is about choosing not to. It's not surrendering; it's shifting. You're saying, "I see what you're trying to do, but I'm not playing by your rules." You stay grounded. You stay steady. You stay aligned with who you know you are, even when someone else is trying to pull you out of character.

There's a quiet kind of strength in that. It's not loud. It doesn't post about revenge or rant about being wronged. It's the kind of strength that holds eye contact, breathes deep, and walks away knowing you didn't lose yourself trying to win a moment.

That's what Jesus modeled over and over again. He stood in front of people who mocked, lied, and insulted Him, and He didn't shrink or lash out. He didn't trade peace for power. He chose restraint because He knew who was really in control.

Turning the other cheek doesn't mean pretending nothing happened. It doesn't mean staying in harmful situations or tolerating mistreatment. It means knowing your response has power. It means understanding that silence can sometimes be stronger than shouting. And it means trusting that God will handle what you don't have to.

It takes real courage to do that. It takes maturity to stay calm when everything in you wants to react. But the more you practice it, the freer you become. Because the truth is, the people trying to provoke you don't control your peace unless you give it to them.

So the next time someone tries to get a reaction out of you, remember this isn't about being passive. It's about being powerful in a way that's unfamiliar to the world. Stand tall. Stay calm. Keep your peace.

That's what it really means to turn the other cheek.

SIXTEEN

Flipping Tables

Everybody loves the story of Jesus flipping tables. It's one of those moments where people breathe a little sigh of relief because finally, Jesus looks angry. Finally, He does something that feels human. But if you really look at what was happening, you'll see that it wasn't about rage. It was about righteousness.

The temple had become something it was never meant to be. It was supposed to be a place of prayer, but people had turned it into a market. A place for profit instead of presence. Jesus walked in, saw what had happened, and refused to stay quiet. He started flipping tables and driving out the chaos. But here's what's important — He didn't do that everywhere He went. He didn't live in a constant state of outrage. He didn't walk around flipping tables in every situation that frustrated Him. He did it when people were abusing what was holy.

That distinction matters. Because a lot of people use that story as an excuse to justify their anger. They'll say, "Even Jesus got mad," as if that gives them a free pass to go off on anyone who crosses them. But what Jesus did wasn't about ego or emotion. It was about protecting the integrity of God's house.

There's a difference between flipping a table out of conviction and flipping one out of pride. One restores order. The other just creates another mess.

The truth is, most of us don't need to flip as many tables as we think we do. We don't need to blast people publicly or argue endlessly online. That doesn't heal anything. Most of the time, it just feeds our need to be right. The kind of strength Jesus showed wasn't impulsive. It was measured. It came from knowing exactly when to speak up and when to stay silent.

Sometimes flipping tables looks less like confrontation and more like clarity. It's choosing to stop participating in conversations that dishonor people. It's drawing boundaries where peace keeps getting violated. It's quietly removing your chair from tables that no longer align with who you're becoming.

And sometimes, flipping tables means building new ones. Inviting people to sit down with you instead of shouting across the room. Creating space for honest conversation, healing, and understanding. That's what Jesus did more often than anything else — He sat at tables with people others refused to eat with. He shared meals with sinners, outcasts, and doubters. He flipped one table to restore holiness, but He sat at dozens to restore hearts.

That's the balance we need to learn. There will be moments in your life where you have to stand up, where silence would be compromise. And there will be other moments where the holier thing to do is to stay seated and talk. Wisdom is knowing the difference.

When you're walking with God, not every offense deserves a reaction. Not every disagreement needs a spectacle. But when something truly violates what's sacred — integrity, justice, compassion, truth — that's when the boldness of Jesus becomes necessary. The key is to let your conviction come from alignment, not emotion.

Flipping tables isn't about burning bridges. It's about clearing space for what's meant to be there. Sometimes you need to disrupt what's been misused to make room for what's right. But once the chaos settles, your calling is still the same as His — to invite people back to the table. To bring truth wrapped in grace. To turn confrontation into conversation.

That's what Jesus modeled. Bold enough to confront corruption, humble enough to share bread with those who didn't deserve it. He wasn't afraid to flip a table when it was necessary, but He never stopped inviting people to sit at His.

Maybe that's what showing up spiritually really looks like — knowing when to stand up and when to sit down, when to speak truth and when to listen, when to clear the table and when to set it again.

SEVENTEEN

Walking With Integrity

Integrity isn't about being perfect. It's about being the same person everywhere you go. It's about closing the gap between what you say and what you do, between who you are in public and who you are when nobody's watching.

Most people think integrity is proven in the big moments — the tests, the temptations, the opportunities to choose right over wrong. And yes, those matter. But real integrity is built in the quiet, ordinary decisions. It's built in the moments when no one is keeping score. It's how you treat the person who can't help you. It's how you handle responsibility when nobody's checking. It's whether your private life would stand up to the same light you shine on others.

Integrity doesn't always make life easier, but it always makes life simpler. You don't have to remember who you pretended to be. You don't have to juggle different versions of yourself.

You just show up as you, fully and consistently. There's peace in that.

The hard part is that integrity will always cost something. Sometimes it costs opportunities. Sometimes it costs relationships. Sometimes it costs approval. But what you gain in exchange is worth far more — you gain credibility with yourself. You start to trust your own reflection again. You stop second-guessing your motives because you know your foundation is solid.

It's easy to talk about faith. It's easy to quote verses and post words about character. But integrity is where all of it gets tested. It's not measured by how loudly you speak truth, but by how quietly you live it.

If you look at Jesus' life, He didn't separate His words from His actions. He didn't just teach forgiveness; He practiced it. He didn't just talk about compassion; He lived it. Even when it cost Him reputation, comfort, or safety, He stayed true to what He knew was right. That's integrity — alignment between belief and behavior.

You can't have peace without it. Because when you compromise your integrity, even in small ways, something inside you knows. You might still succeed on paper, but it won't feel right. There's always that quiet tension that comes from living out of sync with what you believe.

The good news is, integrity isn't about never falling short. It's about how you respond when you do. Everyone misses the mark sometimes. What matters is owning it. Admitting when you've messed up. Making it right where you can. That's how integrity rebuilds itself — not through perfection, but through humility.

And when you walk with integrity long enough, something powerful starts to happen. People begin to trust you even when they disagree with you. They might not always understand your choices, but they'll know your word means something. They'll know your faith isn't a costume you wear when it's convenient.

Integrity also builds spiritual authority. It's what gives weight to your words when you talk about God or faith. Because people can tell the difference between someone who preaches and someone who practices.

There's a quiet kind of influence that comes from consistency. You don't have to announce who you are. You just live it, and over time it speaks for itself.

Walking with integrity doesn't mean you'll always be understood. Sometimes it means choosing peace over popularity. Sometimes it means standing alone. But that's okay, because integrity will always outlast applause.

So as you move through your days, keep asking yourself simple questions. Would I make this decision if nobody ever knew about it? Does this align with who I say I want to be? Would I be proud to tell this story later?

If you can answer yes to those, you're walking in the right direction.

That's integrity. Quiet. Consistent. Whole. The kind of strength that doesn't need to be proven — it's lived.

EIGHTEEN

Forgiveness and Freedom

Forgiveness is one of those words that sounds good in theory but feels impossible in practice. It's easy to talk about letting things go when you're not the one who's been hurt. But when you've been betrayed, lied to, or taken advantage of, the idea of forgiving can feel almost offensive. It sounds like saying what happened didn't matter.

But forgiveness doesn't excuse what happened. It releases *you* from having to carry it.

When Jesus taught about forgiveness, He didn't say it because it's polite. He said it because it's the only way to stay free. Bitterness and resentment don't punish the other person.

They poison your own peace. You can hold on to the anger for as long as you want, but the only person it traps is you.

Forgiveness isn't pretending you're fine. It's deciding you're done being weighed down by something that's already behind you. It's not saying, "That was okay." It's saying, "That no longer gets to own me."

People sometimes wait to forgive until they feel ready. But forgiveness isn't a feeling. It's a decision. And most of the time, the feeling doesn't show up until long after you've made the choice. You may have to make that choice more than once. Some wounds are deep. They take time. Forgiveness isn't a one-time event; it's a process that gets easier as you walk it out.

Think about carrying a heavy bag for miles. The longer you hold it, the heavier it feels. You start adjusting your walk just to manage the weight. You might even forget what it feels like to move freely. That's what unforgiveness does to your soul. It reshapes you around your pain. When you finally set it down, everything feels lighter.

That's what God wants for you. Not because He wants to let people off the hook, but because He wants to unhook you from what's holding you back.

Forgiveness doesn't mean you have to trust someone again. It doesn't mean you have to rebuild a relationship. It just means you're no longer giving that person control over your peace. It means you're choosing to live forward instead of reliving the same story over and over again.

Sometimes the hardest person to forgive is yourself. You replay the things you wish you'd done differently, the words you can't take back, the choices that still haunt you. But grace covers that too. God doesn't hold your past against you, so why keep holding it against yourself? When He said, "It is finished," He meant all of it — the guilt, the shame, the regret. You can stop trying to earn what's already been erased.

Forgiveness isn't weak. It's one of the strongest things you'll ever do. It takes courage to stop fighting battles that don't move you forward. It takes strength to release what your pride still wants to punish. It takes trust to believe that justice doesn't depend on you.

When you forgive, you're not denying the hurt. You're declaring that the hurt doesn't get to define the rest of your story.

And over time, something happens. The weight that once felt impossible starts to fade. You think about that person or situation, and instead of pain, you feel peace. That's how you know you're free.

Forgiveness doesn't erase your history. It just redeems it. It takes what was meant to break you and turns it into something that builds you. And once you've experienced that kind of freedom, you'll never want to carry bitterness again.

So if there's something or someone still living rent-free in your heart, this is your invitation to let it go. Not because they deserve it. But because you do.

That's what real forgiveness is. Not forgetting. Not pretending. Just choosing freedom.

NINETEEN

Serving Others With Purpose

Something shifts when you stop living to protect yourself and start living to serve others. The world tells you that success is about climbing higher, getting more, and staying ahead. But in the Kingdom, the real growth happens when you start looking around instead of just looking up.

Serving isn't about status. It's about spirit.

When Jesus walked the earth, He never once acted like He was above anyone. He washed feet. He ate with people everyone else avoided. He paused for interruptions that others saw as inconveniences. He didn't serve because He had to — He served because it was who He was.

That's what purpose looks like. It's not always grand or glamorous. Most of the time, it's quiet, small, and simple. It's the moments that don't make headlines but change hearts.

For a lot of people, the word "serving" can sound like something heavy. Another obligation to fit in somewhere between work, family, and everything else. But that's not what this is about. Serving isn't something you *have* to do. It's something you *get* to do. It's a way of saying, "God, thank You for what You've given me. Let me pass it on."

When you serve from that place, it stops feeling like a chore. It becomes an act of worship.

The truth is, everyone's called to serve — just not all in the same way. For some, it's helping in obvious ways: feeding the hungry, volunteering, mentoring, giving. For others, it's being present when someone's falling apart. It's showing patience when you'd rather walk away. It's offering encouragement instead of criticism.

Service isn't limited to a title or a platform. It's the way you show up in your world. It's the tone in your voice, the way you listen, the way you choose kindness even when no one's keeping track.

And here's the thing: you don't serve to be seen. You serve because you've seen God. Once you really experience grace, it's hard to keep it to yourself. Gratitude naturally turns into generosity. It's not about proving your faith — it's about expressing it.

Sometimes the most powerful service doesn't look spiritual at all. It's helping a coworker who's struggling without announcing it. It's checking in on someone long after everyone else has moved on. It's forgiving someone and choosing to pray for them instead of gossiping about them. Those are small moments that ripple far beyond what you can see.

Serving with purpose means being intentional about where you pour your energy. Not every need is your assignment. Jesus didn't heal everyone He met, but He was fully present with the ones God put in front of Him. You don't have to save the world. Just be faithful with the people right in front of you.

When you start seeing service this way, it stops feeling like sacrifice and starts feeling like overflow. It's not draining when it's done from a full heart. It's fulfilling.

And the best part is, serving others doesn't just change them — it changes you. It softens your edges. It keeps your pride in check. It reminds you that your life carries weight that's measured in more than money or recognition.

So look around. Who's within reach right now? Where could a small act of kindness make a big difference? What do you already have in your hands that could help someone else stand a little taller?

Serving isn't about what you lose. It's about what you give room to grow.

The world is full of people waiting for proof that God still sees them. When you serve with purpose, you become that proof.

TWENTY

Faith in the Storm

It's easy to talk about faith when everything's going right.
When the bills are paid, the plans are working, and the
prayers are being answered, faith feels natural. But real faith
shows up when life doesn't make sense. When the prayers go
unanswered. When the news hits hard. When you're standing
in the middle of something you never saw coming and the
only thing you can do is breathe and try to believe that God
still has you.

Everyone faces storms. Some hit fast and pass quickly. Others
linger and test every part of who you are. And if you're
honest, sometimes it feels like God's asleep in the boat while
the waves are crashing all around you.

But faith isn't about pretending the storm isn't real. It's about
knowing that even if the waves keep rising, you're not alone
in it.

When the disciples panicked in the storm, Jesus didn't criticize them for being afraid. He reminded them who was with them. The same wind that felt out of control to them was still under His authority. That's what faith looks like — not denying the chaos, but trusting that the same God who calms seas can carry you through them.

Storms have a way of revealing what's built to last. They shake loose what's shallow and force your roots to go deeper. When life is easy, you can convince yourself that you're strong because everything's stable. But when the wind hits, you find out what your foundation's really made of.

That's not punishment. That's strengthening.

Sometimes God calms the storm. Sometimes He calms you and lets the storm keep raging. Either way, His peace is still the promise.

You'll know you're growing when you stop asking, "Why is this happening?" and start asking, "What is this teaching me?" Every storm carries wisdom. Every setback carries shaping. Sometimes the blessing isn't that you avoided the storm — it's that you came through it different. Stronger. Softer. More certain of who God is and who you are.

There will be nights when you still question everything. Times when faith feels paper-thin. Moments when you wonder if God is even listening. Don't let those moments make you feel disqualified. Doubt doesn't mean you've lost faith. It means you're still fighting to hold onto it.

The key is to keep showing up. Keep praying, even when it feels quiet. Keep doing the next right thing, even when you can't see where it's leading. Faith grows in the small steps taken through the fog, not in the big leaps when everything's clear.

And when the storm finally passes — because it will — you'll look back and realize you weren't just surviving. You were being refined. You'll see how certain closed doors made room for better ones. You'll see how strength you didn't know you had was being built in the middle of the struggle. You'll see how the same storm you begged God to take away became the very thing that taught you to trust Him deeper.

Faith doesn't mean you won't get scared. It means you don't let fear steer the ship. You keep moving, keep trusting, keep believing that even when you can't trace His hand, you can still trust His heart.

Because every storm has an end. And when the clouds clear and the sun breaks through, you'll realize that what felt like drowning was really growth — and that the same God who got you through this one will be right there when the next one comes.

That's what it means to have faith in the storm. Not blind optimism. Not denial. Just quiet confidence that no matter how hard it gets, you're never weathering it alone.

TWENTY-ONE

When Bad Things Happen

It's one of the hardest questions in all of faith. If God is good, why do bad things happen?

Why does a child die too young? Why does cancer take someone who spent their life helping others? Why does someone who did everything right still end up broken?

Questions like these have kept more people from trusting God than any sermon ever could. And the truth is, there's no answer that fully satisfies the pain behind them.

But there is perspective.

The Bible says that God is light, and in Him there is no darkness at all. Darkness isn't something He made. It's what happens where His light is rejected or absent.

That's what happened in the very beginning. When sin entered the world, it was like flipping a switch that dimmed the light in everything. Pain, sickness, tragedy, and death weren't part of God's design. They're symptoms of a world living apart from the One who gives it life.

Think about it like this: darkness doesn't exist on its own. It's just the absence of light. You can't turn darkness on. You can only turn the light off.

Evil works the same way. It isn't equal to God or in competition with Him. It's what happens when people and creation operate outside of His will.

That might explain where suffering comes from, but it doesn't make it easy to live through.

When pain hits close to home, theology doesn't always help. What does help is knowing that God doesn't stand far away from it. He stepped into it.

Jesus didn't avoid pain. He entered it. He suffered betrayal, injustice, loss, and even death. He didn't promise us a life free from trouble. He promised His presence through it.

"In this world you will have trouble. But take heart! I have overcome the world." *(John 16:33)*

That verse doesn't make the pain disappear. It just reminds you that pain doesn't get the last word.

When something tragic happens, it's not proof that God stopped being good. It's proof that we still need His goodness to make sense of the brokenness around us.

And even when you can't see what He's doing, He's still working. Romans 8:28 says, "In all things God works for the good of those who love Him." Not that all things are good, but that nothing is beyond redemption.

Sometimes the light looks like a miracle. Other times it looks like comfort, strength, or peace that doesn't make sense. Either way, it's still light, and darkness can't overcome it.

When bad things happen, it's okay to grieve. It's okay to ask questions. It's okay to not understand. Faith doesn't mean pretending everything's fine. It means trusting that even when everything isn't, God still is.

He's not waiting for you to have perfect faith before He meets you in the pain. He's already there. Right in the middle of it.

And while you may never get the explanation you want, what you will get is His presence. And that's what brings healing in the end.

Because even when the world feels dark, the light still shines. And it always wins.

TWENTY-TWO

The Quiet Season

There will come a time in your walk with God when everything goes still.

You'll pray like you always do, but the words feel like they're bouncing off the ceiling. You'll read the Bible, but nothing seems to land. You'll show up to church and sing the songs, but your heart feels flat.

And you'll start to wonder, "Where did He go?"

It's a strange kind of silence — not angry or punishing, just quiet. You haven't turned away. You haven't stopped believing. It just feels like God did.

If you've ever felt that way, you're not broken. You're in what I call the quiet season.

The quiet season is when faith shifts from being something you feel to something you know. It's where trust stops depending on signs, and starts depending on character — His and yours.

Even the people in Scripture faced this. David cried out, "Why, Lord, do You stand far off? Why do You hide Yourself in times of trouble?" The same David who wrote songs of praise also wrote songs of silence.

Jesus felt it too. On the cross He said, "My God, my God, why have You forsaken me?" If the Son of God could experience that distance, it's safe to say the rest of us will too.

But here's what I've learned. Silence doesn't mean absence.

Sometimes God goes quiet not because He's left, but because He's letting you grow. When you're learning to walk, the parent doesn't hold your hand every step. They stay close, but they let you find your balance. That's what the quiet season is. Learning to balance faith when you can't feel it.

There's purpose in the stillness.

It's where roots go deeper. It's where obedience becomes real. Anyone can trust when the answers come quickly and the worship feels alive. But it's in the quiet where your faith learns endurance.

You stop chasing emotional highs and start leaning on eternal truth.

You remember verses like Exodus 14:14 — "The Lord will fight for you; you need only to be still." And Psalm 46:10 — "Be still, and know that I am God."

Stillness is not inactivity. It's intentional trust.

When life feels silent, don't assume you've been abandoned. Assume you're being strengthened. God speaks in many ways, and sometimes His silence says, "You already have what you need."

Keep praying, even when it feels one-sided. Keep showing up, even when you don't sense anything happening. Faith is built in repetition, not reward.

The quiet season will end. It always does. The same voice that spoke the world into motion will speak again. And when He does, you'll recognize it faster, because you learned to listen when there was nothing to hear.

That's the quiet season.

It's not punishment. It's preparation.

And when you walk through it with patience and trust, you come out not just believing *in* God, but believing *with* Him. In rhythm, in sync, and ready for what's next.

TWENTY-THREE

Finding Your Faith Family

Faith was never meant to be a solo journey. From the very beginning, God designed people to grow in community. But somewhere along the way, many of us started trying to do faith alone — maybe because of bad church experiences, mistrust, disappointment, or just plain exhaustion.

If you've ever walked away from church because it felt fake or heavy or judgmental, you're not the only one. A lot of people love God but struggle to find their place among His people. They want connection without the drama. They want honesty without the masks.

The truth is, the church isn't supposed to be a perfect place. It's supposed to be a healing one. And like any family, it can get messy. But even with its flaws, you still need one. Because isolation might feel safe, but it's not sustainable. Faith can survive in solitude for a while, but it grows in fellowship.

Finding your faith family isn't about finding a group that looks or sounds exactly like you. It's about finding people who are chasing the same kind of growth you are — people who pull you higher, who speak truth when it's uncomfortable, and who remind you of who you are when you start to forget.

A real faith family won't always tell you what you want to hear, but they'll love you enough to tell you what you need to. They'll pray for you when you're struggling, celebrate when you win, and check in when you disappear. They'll see your blind spots and still choose to walk beside you.

When you find that, hold on to it.

It might take time. You may visit churches that don't fit. You may meet groups that feel off. That's okay. Keep searching. Don't let one bad experience convince you that belonging isn't for you. The enemy loves to isolate people, because alone is where faith starts to fade. But when you surround yourself with others who believe, their strength starts to cover you when yours feels weak.

And remember, finding your faith family isn't just about what you receive — it's about what you bring. You have something others need too. Your story, your encouragement, your perspective. Every community needs different parts of the body working together. You might be the hand someone else needs to hold. You might be the voice someone else needs to hear.

Church isn't about sitting through a service. It's about showing up as part of something bigger than yourself. It's about creating a rhythm of connection that keeps your faith alive even when life gets hard.

When you find people who remind you of God's goodness, who push you to grow, who lift you up instead of pulling you down — that's your faith family. It doesn't matter if it's a small group, a congregation, a Bible study, or a few close friends who meet for coffee and prayer. What matters is that you keep showing up.

Faith grows best in shared soil.

So if you've been doing this alone, maybe it's time to start looking again. Ask God to guide you to the right people. Be patient while He connects the dots. And when He does, don't stand at the edge — step in.

Because somewhere out there, someone's waiting for you too.

TWENTY-FOUR

Spiritual Mentors and Accountability

No one grows without guidance. Every strong believer you've ever met — the ones who seem grounded, wise, and steady — got there because someone walked with them. None of us were meant to figure faith out alone.

The world tells you that independence is strength, but in the Kingdom, strength looks like teachability. It's knowing when to listen, when to ask questions, and when to let someone who's walked farther than you help point the way.

A spiritual mentor isn't someone who has it all together. It's someone who's learned how to stay close to God through both the good and the bad. They don't just quote Scripture; they live it. You can see it in the way they carry peace through pressure and humility through success.

The right mentor won't just tell you what you want to hear. They'll tell you the truth. They'll ask the hard questions. They'll remind you of who you are when you start acting like someone you're not. That's what real accountability looks like — love that's willing to correct.

Accountability isn't control. It's covering. It's knowing that someone's praying for you, checking in, and holding you steady when you start to drift. It's not about rules or judgment. It's about safety.

But mentorship and accountability only work when they're grounded in humility. You can't learn from someone you're trying to impress. And you can't help someone who won't be honest. The power of mentorship is found in transparency. It's in saying, "Here's where I'm struggling," and letting someone speak truth into it without shame.

The Bible says, "Plans fail for lack of counsel, but with many advisers they succeed." That's not just good advice for business — it's a principle for life. Wisdom grows in conversation. Faith strengthens in community. And accountability keeps you from drifting so far that you forget where you started.

That's why who you let influence you matters. Not everyone who talks about faith should have a say in your growth. Look for fruit, not followers. Pay attention to how someone treats people when no one's watching. Watch how they handle power, money, and correction. A mentor who's still learning is better than a leader who's stopped listening.

And when you find someone who's genuine — who lives what they teach and points you back to God instead of themselves — hold onto that relationship. Ask questions. Be honest. Let them challenge you. Iron sharpens iron, but only if you're willing to make contact.

The truth is, mentorship isn't just about having people above you. It's also about having people beside you and behind you. Someone to guide you, someone to walk with you, and someone you're helping pull forward. That's how faith multiplies — not through performance, but through relationship.

So don't try to do this alone. Find people who make you better. Stay humble enough to learn, and brave enough to be honest. And remember that accountability isn't a cage — it's a safety net that keeps you from falling farther than you have to.

TWENTY-FIVE

Faith for Sale

Let's start with the honest question. If you paid for this book, doesn't that make me part of the same system I'm talking about?

It's a fair question. The difference isn't in whether something costs money. It's in what the money is building.

Money itself isn't holy or unholy. It's directional. It reveals motive. When it moves through someone to reach others, that's stewardship. When it stops with someone to build image or control, that's salesmanship. That's the line.

Real ministry always flows outward. It builds bigger tables, not taller fences. It multiplies what it's been given. It uses resources, attention, and influence to equip others and make space for more people to come in. That's what Jesus modeled.

He never built fences. He built tables. He invited people in —
the broken, the doubters, the forgotten — and He gave freely
to those who couldn't pay Him back.

But when faith gets distorted, that flow reverses. The energy,
attention, and money all start moving toward the person
instead of through them. The message shifts from God's
goodness to the individual's brand. What once pointed to the
cross starts pointing to a logo. That's when faith stops being
ministry and starts becoming marketing.

You can see the difference if you slow down enough to look
for fruit. Real fruit grows quietly. It's steady, not flashy. It
shows up in character, family, and peace. It produces healing,
humility, and gratitude. It's not measured in followers,
revenue, or reach — it's measured in how people's lives
actually change. You'll know you're seeing the real thing when
the work still stands even if the platform disappears.

That's why it's wise to follow the money, not out of suspicion,
but out of discernment. In healthy ministry, resources move
outward. They fund growth, generosity, and community. The
money doesn't sit in one place; it flows through to others.
When money stops moving, it starts molding.

If a mission collapses when the money slows down, it was
never ministry. It was marketing.

And we can't ignore what's happened in modern culture.
People see preachers living like celebrities, flying private,
buying mansions, and asking for "seed offerings" from people

barely getting by. They see churches that look more like concert arenas than sanctuaries and leaders who seem untouchable behind security teams and VIP sections. It's no wonder so many people walk away. To them, faith starts looking like a business model instead of a calling.

That kind of excess doesn't just hurt credibility. It damages hearts. It makes sincere people question whether anyone preaching prosperity actually believes what Jesus said about humility. It makes the whole thing look like a joke to the world. And that's heartbreaking, because real ministry is sacred. It's supposed to heal people, not hustle them.

But before you throw it all away, remember this — extravagance isn't evidence of God's blessing. Jesus never owned much, yet He lacked nothing. The early church didn't have massive buildings or production budgets. They met in homes, shared meals, and gave whatever they had to help each other. The power wasn't in the performance. It was in the purity.

So don't measure faith by what someone drives, wears, or builds. Measure it by what they give away. If the wealth around them multiplies generosity, that's fruit. If it multiplies ego, that's infection.

This is where posture matters most. A real Kingdom heart stays open-handed. It teaches freely, gives freely, and trusts God to provide what's needed. It's not afraid to share space, pass opportunities, or lift up others. A commercial posture does the opposite. It clings. It controls. It treats people like followers instead of family and truth like a trademark instead of a gift.

You can feel the difference even if you can't always explain it. Real ministry feels like invitation. Counterfeit ministry feels like manipulation. One says, "Come and see." The other says, "Look at me."

The real test of it all is simple: what happens when the spotlight goes out? If the work continues, if people keep growing even when the audience isn't watching, that's Kingdom. If everything depends on visibility, it's not faith work — it's image management.

And that brings us back to this book. You paid for it, so how is this different? The truth is, it's not about selling faith. It's about sharing perspective that helps you live it. You're not buying access to God. You're investing in something designed to point you back to Him. The goal isn't for you to depend on my voice. It's for you to hear His more clearly in your own life.

Everything that flows from this work is meant to build bigger tables — to create tools, teaching, and conversations that help more people find freedom and faith. That's the standard I hold myself to, and it's the same one I'd tell you to use for anyone you follow.

If you ever wonder whether someone's message is real, look for the flow. Does it draw people closer to God or closer to them? Does it invite more people in or build walls around who's allowed? Does it release resources into others or hoard them? Does it grow humility or celebrity? Those questions will tell you almost everything you need to know.

The Church has always wrestled with this tension — the pull between calling and comfort, service and spotlight. The answer isn't to walk away from faith. It's to walk with discernment. Be generous, but be wise. Support people who build bigger tables. Sow into work that multiplies good. Be part of things that lift others, not elevate one person.

Because healthy ministry isn't free of money. It's free of manipulation. It doesn't chase wealth; it channels it. It doesn't trade God's name for gain; it uses gain to honor His name.

In the end, truth doesn't need to trend to transform. Faith that's lived will always speak louder than faith that's sold. Real fruit will always outlast the flash.

So keep your heart open, your hands clean, and your eyes on the direction of the flow. That's how you stay part of what's real.

TWENTY-SIX

Holy Excuses

One of the hardest parts about being a person of faith today is watching people use faith to excuse their own behavior. You've probably seen it. Someone lies, manipulates, gossips, or treats people terribly, and when they're called on it, they hide behind a verse or a title.

They'll say things like, "God knows my heart," or "The Holy Spirit told me," when what they really mean is, "I don't want to be corrected."

It's a strange form of spiritual deflection. Instead of letting faith refine them, they use it to protect their pride. And when that happens, it doesn't just hurt their own growth. It hurts everyone watching.

Some people don't walk away from church because they hate God. They walk away because they've seen too many people claiming His name while living the opposite of what He taught.

That's what I call a holy excuse.

A holy excuse is when someone uses their faith as a shield instead of a mirror. They talk about the fruit of the Spirit but refuse to show it. They justify arrogance by calling it confidence. They use the word "discernment" to mask judgment. They twist "standing firm in faith" into "refusing to grow."

And if you want to justify something badly enough, you can almost always find a verse that seems to back you up. That's the danger of reading Scripture through pride instead of humility. The Bible is alive, but when you cherry-pick verses to defend behavior instead of transform it, you turn truth into a weapon.

Even the enemy quoted Scripture to Jesus in the wilderness. That's proof enough that knowing verses isn't the same thing as living them.

But faith isn't meant to make you untouchable. It's meant to make you teachable.

Paul said it clearly in Romans 6: "Should we keep on sinning so that grace may abound? By no means." Grace isn't permission. It's power to live differently.

Real faith will always invite conviction. It welcomes accountability. It changes how you treat people, not just how you talk about God.

Proverbs 12:1 says, "Whoever loves discipline loves knowledge, but whoever hates correction is stupid." It's blunt, but it's true. When you're walking with God, correction isn't an insult. It's a gift.

When people use faith as a scapegoat for their behavior, it creates confusion for everyone else. Nonbelievers start thinking all Christians are hypocrites. People who genuinely want to grow start to question if they even belong. And those watching from a distance walk away from faith altogether because the representation they've seen feels fake.

Jesus warned about that too. He said, "Not everyone who says to me, 'Lord, Lord,' will enter the kingdom of heaven, but only those who do the will of my Father." Faith isn't in the label you wear. It's in the life you live.

But the truth is, when we see this kind of behavior, it stirs something in us. It's easy to want to point it out, expose it, or call it what it is. That's the "table-flipping" instinct we talked about earlier. You see hypocrisy, and you want to fix it fast.

And sometimes, yes, correction is needed. But most of the time, doubling down just makes us bitter. You end up spending more time reacting to bad examples than living as a good one.

Like we talkked about in an earlier chapter, flipping tables has its place, but even Jesus didn't do it every time He saw hypocrisy. He chose His moments carefully, and His heart was always for restoration, not revenge.

That's the balance we have to find. You can recognize hypocrisy without becoming consumed by it. You can call out sin without letting anger shape your spirit. You can hold truth and grace at the same time.

When you see people using faith as a weapon, the best response isn't to fight them with the same one. It's to quietly, consistently live something different. Let your patience, humility, and peace become the proof that faith still works when it's real.

If your faith always makes you feel right but never makes you humble, it's not faith. It's pride wearing a cross.

True holiness doesn't demand excuses. It produces fruit. The kind of fruit that's patient, gentle, and grounded. The kind that draws people closer to God, not pushes them farther away.

Faith was never meant to be a scapegoat. It was meant to be a standard. A reminder of how to live, not a reason to avoid responsibility.

When people misuse faith to justify their words or their wounds, they might win arguments, but they lose influence. The world doesn't need louder believers. It needs truer ones.

And if you've ever been turned off by people like this, hear me clearly. That's not what Jesus looks like. What you're rejecting isn't God. It's a distorted version of Him.

So let's not use faith as an excuse for our flaws. And let's not let someone else's misuse of faith harden our hearts either.

Faith that hides behind excuses will always push people away. But faith that takes ownership, stays teachable, and keeps showing grace will always bring them closer.

TWENTY-SEVEN

Iron Sharpens Iron

Faith was never meant to be a solo sport. You can believe alone, pray alone, and even grow alone for a season, but real transformation happens in connection. The people you walk with shape the person you become.

Proverbs says, "As iron sharpens iron, so one person sharpens another." It's a verse that sounds encouraging until you really think about it — because sharpening means friction. It means contact. It means that sometimes sparks will fly. You don't get sharper by staying comfortable.

The right people in your life won't just agree with you. They'll refine you. They'll tell you when you're out of line, pray with you when you're struggling, and remind you of your calling when you start losing focus. Real friends won't let you drift quietly away from who you're supposed to be.

That's what "iron sharpens iron" really looks like — not constant correction, but honest conversation. Not competition, but accountability. It's two people walking together and saying, "I'm for you, but I'm also for your growth."

It's easy to surround yourself with people who make you feel good. It's harder to surround yourself with people who make you better. But the truth is, comfort doesn't change you. Challenge does.

Healthy sharpening relationships always have mutual respect. It's not about control. It's not about one person being the expert. It's about shared pursuit. Two people chasing the same God, both trying to live with integrity, both willing to be honest.

And honesty doesn't mean harshness. It's not about pointing out every flaw. It's about caring enough to speak truth even when it's uncomfortable. It's choosing relationship over reputation. It's saying, "I love you enough to tell you this," and meaning it.

If you've ever had someone tell you something that stung at first but helped you grow later, that's sharpening. It hurts in the moment, but it leaves you better than it found you. And if you've ever been that person for someone else, you know it takes courage. You risk being misunderstood. You risk tension. But love without truth isn't love — it's comfort.

The other side of sharpening is humility. You can't be sharpened if you're too proud to admit you have dull edges. Everyone does. We all have blind spots, habits, or mindsets that only other people can help us see. God uses community to polish us. The friction isn't failure; it's formation.

But not every relationship sharpens you. Some drain you. Some dull you. That's why discernment matters. Pay attention to how you feel after spending time with people. Do you leave encouraged, convicted, and focused? Or do you leave anxious, small, and off balance?

The right people will call you higher, not pull you lower. They'll challenge your decisions but still believe in your purpose. They'll correct you privately and defend you publicly. That's the kind of people you need in your corner.

If you want to keep your edge spiritually, stay close to people who keep theirs. Don't isolate when you're struggling — that's when you need sharpening the most.

And if you're the one doing the sharpening, do it with grace. Be patient. Remember that iron doesn't break iron — it strengthens it. The goal isn't to win the argument. It's to win your brother or sister back to truth.

When believers learn how to sharpen each other the right way, community becomes powerful again. It stops being a popularity contest and becomes a partnership in purpose.

So ask yourself who sharpens you — and who you're sharpening in return. If the answer is no one, start there. Find your people. Build that circle. Be the kind of friend who tells the truth gently, listens deeply, and prays faithfully.

Because in the end, dull blades can't cut through anything. But when iron meets iron in love and truth, sparks might fly — and that's where the light comes from.

TWENTY-EIGHT

Faith at Home

Faith starts where you live. It's not proven on a stage, or online, or in front of strangers — it's proven in the small moments that happen behind closed doors.

It's easy to look strong in public. It's easy to post verses, talk about grace, and act humble around people who only see one side of you. But your real faith shows up in how you treat the people who see every side.

Your home is your first ministry. The way you love your family, the way you lead through stress, the way you handle disagreement — that's where your faith gets tested and revealed.

For a lot of people, this is where the gap shows up. You can spend all day serving, encouraging, and helping others, but if you come home angry, distant, or disengaged, something's off. The truth is, it's easier to be patient with strangers than with the people closest to you. But that's exactly why home matters so much. It's the place where faith either becomes real or stays a performance.

When Scripture talks about leading your household well, it's not about control or perfection. It's about presence. It's about showing up. It's about being the same person in your house that you claim to be everywhere else.

Your family doesn't need a preacher. They need an example. They need to see what peace looks like when the bills are tight. They need to see what humility looks like when you're wrong. They need to see what grace looks like when someone messes up.

You can't teach faith at home through words alone. You teach it through tone, through consistency, through how you respond under pressure. Kids especially learn by imitation. They'll follow your actions long before they understand your explanations.

You don't have to get it perfect. You just have to be honest. If you lose your temper, apologize. If you're scared, talk about it. If you're praying through something, let them see that too. Authenticity is what builds trust. Pretending to have it all together only teaches people to hide when they don't.

Faith at home also means creating space for conversation. Don't make prayer or Bible reading feel like a lecture. Make it part of normal life. Ask questions at the dinner table. Share stories of how you've seen God show up in your own day. Invite everyone's perspective.

It's not about forcing faith — it's about planting seeds. When you make it natural, people lean in. When you make it forced, they check out.

And remember, your spouse, kids, or loved ones might be on different parts of their faith journey. That's okay. The goal isn't to drag them to where you are. It's to walk together, to show grace, and to trust that God is working on them the same way He's working on you.

When your home becomes a place of peace instead of performance, everything changes. The walls start to breathe again. Conversations soften. Trust rebuilds. You stop needing your family to see you as perfect and start letting them see you as real.

Because faith isn't just something you carry into the world — it's something you cultivate in the people closest to you. It's not about being the head of the house in title. It's about being the heart of it in practice.

So before you try to change the world, start by loving your home well. Pray together. Listen more than you correct. Celebrate small wins. Lead with peace. Let your family feel the fruit of your faith, not just hear about it.

Because if faith doesn't work at home, it doesn't work anywhere.

TWENTY-NINE

Faith at Work

Faith isn't meant to stay at home or in church. It's meant to walk into every room you do — including your workplace.

For a lot of people, this is where the tension starts. You want to live your faith, but you don't want to force it on anyone. You want to represent what you believe, but you also want to keep your job. It can feel like you have to choose between being bold and being quiet, between living what you believe and blending in.

But living your faith at work isn't about preaching sermons. It's about living one.

You don't need to quote verses at every meeting or correct every coworker who doesn't share your views. You just need to show up with integrity, kindness, and consistency. The way you lead. The way you listen. The way you handle stress and treat people who can't do anything for you — those are sermons people actually remember.

Jesus didn't say people would know His followers by their ability to argue. He said they'd know them by their love.

That's how faith at work comes to life. It's showing grace when someone makes a mistake. It's staying calm when everyone else is panicking. It's refusing to gossip, even when the conversation makes it easy. It's doing your job with excellence, not because you're being watched, but because you see your work as worship.

If you treat your work as something sacred, it changes how you approach it. You stop cutting corners. You stop complaining as much. You stop separating "spiritual" and "secular." Every assignment, every customer, every task becomes an opportunity to honor God by how you carry yourself.

That doesn't mean it's easy. The workplace can test your patience like nothing else. You'll deal with difficult people, unfair expectations, and days where faith feels far away. But that's where it matters most. That's where people actually see the difference.

Because faith that only works when everything's peaceful isn't faith — it's preference.

You can also carry faith at work by being someone who lifts others up. Encourage people. Celebrate their wins. Listen when they need to vent. You don't have to mention God's name every time to reflect His nature. The presence of peace in a chaotic environment speaks louder than a thousand verses out of context.

And when someone does ask where your peace comes from, be ready to answer simply and sincerely. You don't have to convince them of anything. Just tell the truth. "Honestly, my faith helps me stay grounded." That's it. No pressure. No performance. Just presence.

There's a difference between sharing your faith and selling it. You share it by living it — consistently, quietly, without expecting anything in return.

If you ever feel discouraged that your workplace doesn't feel "spiritual," remember that Jesus spent most of His life doing ordinary work. Before He ever preached a sermon, He built tables and fixed chairs. The sacred and the simple were never separate for Him.

So whether you're leading a team, serving customers, or doing something that no one ever notices, your work still matters. Your faith can live there. Your light can shine there. And sometimes, the best ministry you'll ever do is how you handle the parts of life that feel the least spiritual.

Faith at work doesn't mean you have to be loud about what you believe. It means you're loyal to it — in your attitude, your honesty, and your effort.

Because if you can live your faith in the place that tests your patience, you can live it anywhere.

THIRTY

Sharing Your Faith Authentically

For a lot of people, faith conversations feel uncomfortable. You don't want to come across as preachy or pushy, but you also don't want to hide what matters most to you. And on the flip side, there are people who charge in with Bible verses and bold declarations, thinking they're helping — but what they're really doing is pushing people farther away.

Somewhere along the line, a lot of believers started confusing boldness with volume. But being loud about your faith doesn't make it more real.

Jesus never forced belief. He invited it.

He didn't walk around condemning people. He met them where they were. He looked them in the eyes. He listened. He told stories that helped them see truth for themselves. And even when people disagreed with Him, they still wanted to be around Him. That's what authenticity looks like — living in a way that draws people in, not drives them off.

When you share your faith authentically, you're not performing. You're not trying to win an argument or prove your righteousness. You're simply opening a window into your own story — what God has done in your life, how He's met you in moments of doubt, how your faith has carried you through what didn't make sense. People can debate theology all day long, but they can't debate your experience.

That's why vulnerability always beats volume.

When you lead with honesty instead of superiority, something beautiful happens — people start to listen. Because the truth is, most people aren't rejecting Jesus. They're rejecting the way they've seen Him represented.

The loudest faith isn't always the strongest one. Sometimes the most powerful witness is quiet consistency. It's showing kindness to the coworker everyone else ignores. It's forgiving someone who doesn't deserve it. It's staying calm when the world expects you to lose it. Those moments preach louder than any sermon you could ever speak.

If you ever feel the urge to "correct" someone into belief, pause. Ask yourself whether you're trying to win them to God or win them to your side. There's a difference. People can feel the difference. When love is the motive, it lands differently.

Authentic faith doesn't judge from a distance. It sits down. It listens. It remembers that everyone's story is still unfolding. You don't have to rush someone's process or pressure them to arrive where you are. Just be present. Let your life be the evidence.

And when the moment comes to speak, keep it simple. No script, no agenda. Just share the truth of what God's done in you. Maybe it's a sentence. Maybe it's a story. Maybe it's just, "I've been there, and I found peace that didn't make sense."

That's what invites people closer — not polished words, but genuine presence.

The goal of sharing your faith isn't to close the deal. It's to open the door.

Because when people feel seen, they start to trust. And once trust is there, truth can follow.

So don't worry about having the right words. Live a life that makes people curious about where your peace comes from. Let your actions prepare the ground for your words, and when you do speak, let love do the heavy lifting.

You don't have to be loud to be light.

And the world doesn't need more people lecturing about Jesus — it needs more people living like Him.

THIRTY-ONE

Discipleship in Real Life

Discipleship is one of those words that sounds intimidating. It can make people picture classes, handbooks, and church programs with step-by-step instructions. But at its core, discipleship just means helping someone grow closer to God while you keep growing too. It's not about hierarchy. It's about relationship.

When Jesus said, "Go and make disciples," He wasn't talking about forming a club or a curriculum. He was talking about walking with people. Teaching through conversation. Modeling truth through daily life. Most of His lessons didn't happen in temples — they happened around campfires, on dusty roads, and over shared meals.

Discipleship in real life looks the same way. It's not about having all the answers. It's about being available. It's about showing up for people who are hungry for hope, curious about faith, or just trying to make sense of their own story. You don't have to be a pastor to disciple someone. You just have to care enough to walk beside them.

That means listening more than you lecture. Asking more questions than you answer. Encouraging people when they fall, reminding them of grace, and helping them see that growth is rarely linear. It's not a straight climb upward. It's two steps forward, one step back, and a whole lot of mercy in between.

Real discipleship isn't about cloning your faith journey in someone else. It's about helping them discover their own relationship with God. The goal isn't to make them think like you. It's to help them think *with* God.

That's where a lot of people get it wrong. They try to create followers instead of fellow travelers. But the best discipleship is mutual. You learn from each other. You grow together. You hold each other accountable. It's iron sharpening iron — but with patience and grace built in.

There's also something powerful about simply letting people see your process. Don't hide your doubts, your mistakes, or your struggles. Be honest about them. The people you're helping will grow more from watching you wrestle honestly than from hearing you act like you have it all figured out. Vulnerability builds credibility.

And it's okay if it feels messy. It's supposed to. Growth always is. When you walk with someone long enough, you'll both realize that discipleship isn't about perfection. It's about direction. You don't need to be ahead of them in every way. You just need to keep moving toward Jesus together.

Sometimes discipleship looks like weekly coffee and prayer. Sometimes it looks like text messages checking in. Sometimes it's just staying present through hard seasons, being the steady person in a world that keeps shifting.

If you want to know whether you're discipling well, look at the fruit. Are the people around you becoming more confident in God's voice and less dependent on yours? Are they learning to pray, discern, and make decisions for themselves? If so, you're doing it right.

Discipleship done well eventually makes you unnecessary. And that's the point.

Jesus didn't hold His followers hostage to His presence. He equipped them to carry it forward. He said, "Greater things will you do." That's what you're called to — not to build fans, but to build foundations.

So don't overcomplicate it. You don't need a title or a strategy. You just need a heart that says, "Come walk with me for a while. Let's figure this out together."

That's discipleship. Real life. Real love. Real growth.

THIRTY-TWO

Purpose and Calling

One of the biggest questions people wrestle with is, "What's my purpose?" Everyone wants to know why they're here and what they're meant to do with their life. It's the question that can keep you up at night, scrolling through other people's highlight reels, wondering if you somehow missed your turn.

But purpose isn't something you find outside of yourself. It's something you uncover inside of you. It's not hiding on a mountaintop or waiting in a dream job. It's been there since the beginning, placed there by the same hands that formed you.

When God designed you, He didn't make a mistake. He didn't forget to include direction. Every part of your personality, every passion, every experience — even the painful ones — are part of your calling.

We tend to overcomplicate purpose. We chase big titles, big stages, or big recognition. But your calling doesn't have to be big to be holy. Purpose isn't about scale. It's about surrender. It's about waking up each day and asking, "God, how can You use what's in my hands right now?"

Sometimes your calling will look exciting. Sometimes it will look ordinary. You might be building businesses, raising kids, leading teams, or helping quietly behind the scenes. It all matters. Because purpose isn't a position. It's a posture. It's choosing to serve wherever you are, however you can, with whatever you've been given.

That's why it's dangerous to compare callings. What God built in someone else won't fit you, and that's a good thing. The world doesn't need another version of them. It needs you — fully alive in what only you can bring.

Calling also changes with seasons. What you're meant to do at twenty might not be what you're called to do at forty. God doesn't reveal your whole blueprint at once because He wants you to keep walking with Him. Each chapter unfolds a little more of the plan.

You might not realize it, but you're probably already living part of your purpose. It's in the things that make you come alive, the problems you can't stop thinking about, the moments where serving feels natural instead of forced. That's not coincidence — that's calling.

The key to walking in it isn't striving. It's surrender. You don't have to chase purpose. You have to cooperate with it. Ask God to show you where He's already working and how you can join Him there. When you stop forcing it and start flowing with it, peace follows.

There's also a myth that purpose always feels good. It doesn't. Sometimes it's hard. Sometimes it stretches you past your comfort zone. But even when it's hard, it still feels *right*. That's how you know you're where you're supposed to be — not because it's easy, but because it's meaningful.

Purpose isn't something you figure out once and then you're done. It's a relationship. It grows as you do. It requires faith to take the next step even when you can't see the next five. It requires trust that God's timing isn't a delay — it's preparation.

And when you finally start living it, you'll realize that purpose was never about you in the first place. It was about people. Every calling connects to service. God blesses you so that you can bless others. The moment you start using your gifts to lift someone else, you're walking in your calling whether you realize it or not.

So stop waiting for the perfect sign. You don't need one. The same God who created you is guiding you. Keep showing up. Keep doing the work in front of you with excellence and faith. Keep trusting that even the smallest things can have eternal impact.

You were created on purpose and for a purpose. You don't have to find it. You just have to live it — one obedient step at a time.

THIRTY-THREE

Letting Your Light Shine

For a lot of people, the hardest part of faith isn't believing in God — it's believing they have something worth offering on His behalf. They worry about standing out, about looking prideful, about what people might think. So they hide their gifts, soften their voice, or shrink back to avoid attention. But you weren't created to blend in. You were created to shine.

Jesus said, "You are the light of the world. A city on a hill cannot be hidden." He didn't say *try* to be light. He said *you are*. That means your life carries influence whether you realize it or not. The question isn't whether you're shining. The question is what your light is showing.

Letting your light shine doesn't mean walking around trying to prove something. It's not about spotlighting yourself or constantly talking about how spiritual you are. It's about living in such a way that people can see the difference without you having to announce it.

Light doesn't have to explain itself. It just has to exist.

You don't turn on a lamp and hear it give a speech about being bright. It just quietly changes the room. That's what your life is meant to do. You don't have to be loud or perfect to make an impact. You just have to be genuine.

Every time you show kindness when you could have been cold, you shine. Every time you stay calm when others lose it, you shine. Every time you choose grace over gossip, honesty over ease, forgiveness over revenge — you shine.

And the best part is, your light doesn't have to look like anyone else's. God wired you differently on purpose. Some people shine through words. Others through creativity, leadership, empathy, or service. Whatever form it takes, the goal isn't comparison. It's contribution.

Sometimes people dim their light because they think humility means hiding. But humility isn't denying your gifts — it's recognizing their source. It's saying, "Everything good in me came from God, so I'm going to use it for Him." Hiding your light doesn't make you humble. It makes you less effective.

The world doesn't need more people who play small to stay comfortable. It needs people who walk confidently in who God made them to be — not arrogant, just available. When you let your light shine, you're giving other people permission to do the same.

And sometimes, shining looks like simply showing up when you don't feel ready. It looks like saying yes to the conversation, yes to the opportunity, yes to the assignment that scares you. God rarely calls you when you feel qualified. He calls you when you're willing. Because He knows the world needs the light only you can bring.

Of course, shining isn't always easy. The brighter the light, the clearer the shadows around it. You'll face criticism, misunderstanding, and moments of doubt. That's okay. Don't hide because someone else feels uncomfortable with your confidence. Just keep shining with humility and grace.

Light doesn't fight darkness. It reveals it. It brings clarity, warmth, and hope. You don't have to fix every broken thing. You just have to be who you were created to be — a reflection of God's goodness in the spaces you occupy.

So wherever you go today, bring your light with you. Don't overthink it. Don't filter it. Just live honestly, love deeply, and keep pointing back to the One who gave you your glow in the first place.

Because when your life shines, people don't just see you — they see Him.

THIRTY-FOUR

Legacy of Faith

Legacy isn't about what you leave behind. It's about who you leave behind.

Most people think of legacy in terms of achievements — the business they built, the name they made, the wealth they passed on. But those things fade. Time erases titles, money moves hands, and buildings eventually crumble. What endures is the impact your life had on the hearts around you.

Faith has always been generational. The way you live today ripples forward farther than you'll ever see. The way you love, the way you forgive, the way you show grace in hard moments — those things don't stop when you're gone. They take root in other people and keep growing.

That's what a legacy of faith looks like. It's the kind of life that makes it easier for the next person to believe.

You don't have to be famous or powerful to leave that kind of mark. You just have to be faithful. Legacy isn't built in grand gestures. It's built in quiet consistency. It's built in showing up for people when it would be easier not to. It's built in doing what's right even when nobody notices.

When people look back on your life, they won't remember every success. They'll remember how they felt when they were around you. Did they feel seen? Encouraged? Did they feel peace when you walked into the room? Did they see what faith looks like when it's lived instead of preached?

That's what lasts.

And legacy doesn't start someday. It starts now. Every decision, every word, every act of love becomes part of the story you're writing. You're shaping someone's idea of God every time they watch you handle a hard moment with grace. You're teaching what faith looks like every time you forgive, serve, or stay steady when others would fall apart.

You might not even realize it, but someone is watching your walk and finding courage for their own. Someone is quietly learning that they can endure because you did. That's legacy in motion.

A legacy of faith isn't about perfection. It's about perseverance. It's not about never falling — it's about always getting back up and trusting that God can use every stumble for good.

The most powerful legacies don't come from people who lived flawless lives. They come from people who lived surrendered ones. People who kept showing up, kept growing, kept believing that God wasn't done yet.

If you want to build that kind of legacy, focus less on being remembered and more on being real. Love people well. Give freely. Tell the truth. Admit when you're wrong. Be quick to listen and slow to judge. Keep your heart soft and your hands open.

Your life is a message someone else will read after you're gone. Make it one that points to grace.

Because in the end, faith doesn't end with you. It keeps moving — through your kids, your friends, your work, your kindness, your prayers. It outlives your name. It multiplies quietly in the lives you've touched.

That's the legacy that matters.

You don't have to chase it. You just have to live it.

THIRTY-FIVE

The Daily Decision

Faith isn't something you master. It's something you practice.

Every day, you wake up with a choice. You can move through the motions, doing what's safe and familiar. Or you can show up spiritually, choosing presence over distraction, trust over control, and purpose over noise.

The truth is, you're never going to feel perfectly ready for it. Some days faith will feel natural. Other days it will feel like a fight. But that's okay. Showing up spiritually isn't about perfection. It's about consistency. It's about choosing to meet with God again and again, even when your feelings haven't caught up yet.

Faith is a muscle, and it only grows when it's used. You build it in small, steady moments. In prayer before the day begins.

In the decision to forgive. In the quiet act of generosity no one sees. Those moments may not look like much, but they shape everything.

And when you add them up over time, you start to see something forming: strength, peace, and trust. The kind of inner foundation that holds steady even when life doesn't.

There will always be distractions trying to pull you off course. There will be seasons where you drift, and others where you feel like you're walking through fog. But faith isn't about staying perfectly on track. It's about always finding your way back.

Showing up spiritually means learning to live with awareness that God is already present in the ordinary, the quiet, the chaos, and the beauty. It's realizing you don't have to chase Him down. You just have to slow down enough to notice He's been with you the whole time.

You don't have to do big things to grow in faith. You just have to keep saying yes to the small moments of obedience that keep your heart aligned with His.

Pray when you can. Pause when you need to. Trust when you don't understand. Love when it's inconvenient. Forgive when it's undeserved. Serve when no one's watching. Those are the decisions that form your faith over a lifetime.

And on the days when you don't feel spiritual at all, remember this: faith isn't built on your feelings. It's built on His faithfulness. You keep showing up, not because you always see the results, but because you know the One you're showing up for.

The promise you carry isn't that life will be easy. It's that God will always be with you in it. Every sunrise is another invitation to trust Him again. Every breath is proof that He's not finished with you yet.

So take what you've learned here and start living it. One moment at a time. One choice at a time.

Because faith isn't about the big moments that make headlines. It's about the quiet decisions that make history.

Keep showing up. Keep shining. Keep building a life that reflects what you believe, not just in church, but in every slice of who you are.

That's how you strengthen your faith. That's how you live it every day.

That's how you show up more spiritually.

THIRTY-SIX

Scripture Index

This section was written to show you where the truths in this book come from. Not from opinion or theory, but from the Word itself. I didn't want to fill every chapter with verse numbers and footnotes because faith isn't meant to read like a textbook. But here, I want you to see the foundation. These are the Scriptures that shaped what you just read and keep shaping me every day.

Meet the Trinity

When I talked about God as Father, Son, and Holy Spirit, that wasn't an idea I came up with. That's how God describes Himself. Jesus told His followers, "Go and make disciples of all nations, baptizing them in the name of the Father and of the Son and of the Holy Spirit." *(Matthew 28:19)* He also promised that the Holy Spirit would come to guide and teach us.

"But the Helper, the Holy Spirit, whom the Father will send in My name, He will teach you all things and remind you of everything I have said to you." *(John 14:26)* Paul wrote it beautifully at the end of his letter to the Corinthians: "The grace of the Lord Jesus Christ, the love of God, and the fellowship of the Holy Spirit be with you all." *(2 Corinthians 13:14)*

That's the fullness of God. Not parts competing for attention, but one perfect relationship that invites you into it.

Relationship Over Religion

When I said faith is about relationship, not rules, that came straight from Jesus' own words. He often called out people who looked holy on the outside but were disconnected from God's heart. In Matthew 23, He said they focused on appearances while ignoring justice, mercy, and faithfulness. The prophet Micah said it long before that:

"He has shown you, O man, what is good. And what does the Lord require of you? To act justly, to love mercy, and to walk humbly with your God." *(Micah 6:8)* And when Jesus told His disciples, "I no longer call you servants, because a servant does not know his master's business. Instead, I have called you friends." *(John 15:15)* He made it clear that God doesn't want distance. He wants connection.

Hearing the Holy Spirit

When I talked about how the Holy Spirit usually speaks in whispers, not thunder, that picture comes straight from

Elijah's story. He waited to hear God in the wind, the earthquake, and the fire. None of those were it. Then came a gentle whisper. *(1 Kings 19:11–12)* That's still how God speaks. Jesus said, "The Helper, the Holy Spirit, whom the Father will send in My name, will teach you all things and remind you of everything I have said to you." *(John 14:26)* And Paul wrote, "Those who are led by the Spirit of God are the children of God." *(Romans 8:14)* You don't need fireworks to know the Spirit is near. You just need stillness.

Discerning God's Voice

When I wrote about learning to tell God's voice apart from all the others, I wanted to make it clear that discernment isn't just a feeling. It's a practice rooted in Scripture. God never intended for you to walk in confusion. He gave you His Word, His Spirit, and His peace as your guide.

Jesus said,

"My sheep listen to my voice; I know them, and they follow me." John 10:27

That verse tells us two things. First, that God really does speak to His people. And second, that His voice is recognizable when you've spent time with Him. The more you walk with Him, the more familiar His sound becomes.

One of the clearest ways to test what you're hearing is to compare it to Scripture. God's voice will never contradict His Word. The Spirit's role is to remind you of what Jesus already said, not rewrite it.

"The Helper, the Holy Spirit, whom the Father will send in my name, will teach you all things and remind you of everything I have said to you." *John 14:26*

That's how you know what's true. The Spirit always points back to Jesus.

I mentioned that God's voice carries peace, not pressure. That comes from Philippians 4:7, where Paul says,

"The peace of God, which transcends all understanding, will guard your hearts and your minds in Christ Jesus." *Philippians 4:7*

If what you're sensing leads you toward panic, urgency, or pride, it's not Him. His direction brings clarity, not chaos.

Isaiah described that inner guidance perfectly when he said,

"Whether you turn to the right or to the left, your ears will hear a voice behind you, saying, 'This is the way; walk in it.'" *Isaiah 30:21*

That verse shows that discernment isn't about hearing loud commands. It's about staying close enough to sense His direction.

Even when the enemy tried to twist Scripture in the wilderness, Jesus didn't get defensive. He simply answered with truth. That's why knowing the Word matters so much. It protects you from being deceived by something that sounds holy but isn't.

"Then Jesus was led by the Spirit into the wilderness to be tempted by the devil." *(Matthew 4:1–11)*

Every time you take what you hear and hold it up against God's Word, His peace, and His character, your discernment grows sharper.

That's how you learn to know His voice with confidence — by walking closely enough that anything else just sounds off.

Understanding Your Enemy

When I wrote about learning to recognize your enemy, I wanted to make sure you understood two things. First, Satan is real. Second, he's already defeated. The Bible doesn't describe him as God's equal or as a rival force that balances good and evil. He's a created being who rebelled against the Creator.

"How you have fallen from heaven, morning star, son of the dawn! You have been cast down to the earth, you who once laid low the nations." *Isaiah 14:12*

"You were blameless in your ways from the day you were created till wickedness was found in you." *Ezekiel 28:15*

Those verses describe his fall. Pride and rebellion turned beauty into corruption. God didn't lose control; He removed what couldn't stay in His presence.

Jesus confirmed that same truth when He said,

"I saw Satan fall like lightning from heaven." *Luke 10:18*

That line isn't poetic—it's positional. It means the enemy has already been cast down. He still works to deceive, but his authority is limited.

The way he operates hasn't changed since the beginning. In the garden he twisted what God said, asking, "Did God really say...?" (Genesis 3:1). In the wilderness he tried to use Scripture itself to manipulate Jesus (Matthew 4:1–11). In both cases, his strategy was confusion.

That's why knowing truth matters so much. Ephesians 6:11–17 calls it the armor of God—truth, righteousness, peace, faith, salvation, and the Word. Those aren't just words; they're your protection.

"Put on the full armor of God, so that you can take your stand against the devil's schemes." *Ephesians 6:11*

James gives the simplest battle plan there is.

"Submit yourselves, then, to God. Resist the devil, and he will flee from you." *James 4:7*

Submission comes first. When you stay close to God, the enemy loses influence. Light exposes lies, and darkness can't survive exposure.

John said it best:

"The light shines in the darkness, and the darkness has not overcome it." *John 1:5*

That's the foundation of this chapter. You don't need to fear the enemy or obsess over his every move. You just need to stay connected to the light that already defeated him.

When you live in truth, you walk in victory. Darkness doesn't stand a chance.

Divine Design

When I talked about how you were created on purpose, with purpose, that idea comes straight from the Word. You weren't an accident or an afterthought. Scripture says, "You created my inmost being. You knit me together in my mother's womb. I praise you because I am fearfully and wonderfully made." *(Psalm 139:13–14)*

Paul wrote, "For we are God's handiwork, created in Christ Jesus to do good works, which God prepared in advance for us to do." *(Ephesians 2:10)* That means your purpose isn't something you have to chase down. It's something God already built into you.

And when it feels like you're not there yet, Philippians 1:6 reminds us that God finishes what He starts.

"He who began a good work in you will carry it on to completion until the day of Christ Jesus."

You don't have to figure it all out. You just have to keep walking with the One who made you.

Grace Over Guilt

When I wrote about guilt being a treadmill and grace being an open road, I wanted you to remember that guilt keeps you trying to earn what God already gave. Paul said it best.

"For it is by grace you have been saved, through faith. And this is not from yourselves, it is the gift of God, not by works, so that no one can boast." *(Ephesians 2:8–9)*

You don't have to work for grace. You just have to receive it.

And if you've ever wondered whether your past disqualifies you, remember Romans 8:1.

"There is now no condemnation for those who are in Christ Jesus."

God isn't keeping score. He's calling you forward. Even Paul, who carried regret and weakness, heard God say,

"My grace is sufficient for you, for my power is made perfect in weakness." *(2 Corinthians 12:9)*

Grace doesn't erase your story. It redeems it.

Learning to Trust Again

When I wrote about rebuilding trust, I was thinking about how hard it is to believe again after being disappointed or hurt. God never rushes that process. Scripture reminds us that trust isn't something you force. It's something that grows when you see His faithfulness over time.

"Trust in the Lord with all your heart and lean not on your own understanding." *Proverbs 3:5–6*

That verse isn't asking you to ignore logic or shut off your emotions. It's an invitation to stop carrying what you were never meant to control.

David understood that kind of trust. His life was full of betrayal and loss, yet he wrote about how God remained constant when everyone else walked away.

"Even if my father and mother abandon me, the Lord will hold me close." *Psalm 27:10*

That's not just comfort. It's identity. It means that no matter who failed you, God won't.

Job's story shows that trust can survive even when everything else falls apart. After losing nearly everything, Job still said:

"Though he slay me, yet will I hope in him." *Job 13:15*

That kind of faith doesn't come from ignoring pain. It comes from believing that God's goodness is bigger than what you understand right now.

And Isaiah offers one more reminder of why you can keep trusting, even when you don't see the full picture yet.

"You will keep in perfect peace those whose minds are steadfast, because they trust in you." *Isaiah 26:3*

Trust isn't built on perfect outcomes. It's built on perfect character.

When you take small steps to trust God again, you're not pretending the past didn't hurt. You're choosing to believe that He's still good in the middle of it. That's where healing begins.

How to Pray

Prayer was never meant to be a performance. When I said it's as simple as talking to a friend, that came from Jesus Himself. He told His followers,

"When you pray, say: Our Father in heaven, hallowed be your name..." *(Matthew 6:9–13)* He didn't teach a formula. He taught relationship.

Paul later said, "Do not be anxious about anything, but in every situation, by prayer and petition, with thanksgiving, present your requests to God." *(Philippians 4:6)* You don't have to sound holy to be heard. You just have to be honest.

And when you wonder if you're praying the right way, Paul gives one more reminder.

"Pray continually, give thanks in all circumstances, for this is God's will for you in Christ Jesus." *(1 Thessalonians 5:16–18)*

Prayer isn't about getting it right. It's about showing up.

Reading the Word With Purpose

When I wrote about reading the Bible to listen, not just to check a box, I meant that Scripture is alive. It's not meant to be skimmed for quotes. It's meant to be heard. Paul told Timothy,

"All Scripture is God-breathed and is useful for teaching, rebuking, correcting and training in righteousness." *(2 Timothy 3:16–17)*

Psalm 119:105 says,

"Your word is a lamp for my feet, a light on my path." That means you don't need to see the whole road. Just enough to take the next step.

And James reminds us that it's not about information. It's about transformation.

"Do not merely listen to the word, and so deceive yourselves. Do what it says." *(James 1:22)*

Reading the Word isn't about finishing a chapter. It's about letting the chapter finish its work in you.

Worship as a Way of Life

When I talked about worship being more than music, I wanted to remind you that it's about how you live, not just what you sing. Paul said,

"Offer your bodies as a living sacrifice, holy and pleasing to God. This is your true and proper worship." *(Romans 12:1)*

Jesus told the woman at the well that true worship isn't about where you are, but how you come.

"The true worshipers will worship the Father in spirit and in truth, for they are the kind of worshipers the Father seeks." *(John 4:23–24)*

And Paul wrote again,

"Whatever you do, in word or deed, do it all in the name of the Lord Jesus, giving thanks to God the Father through Him." *(Colossians 3:17)*

Worship starts when the song ends. It's a posture, not a playlist.

Hearing God in the Quiet

When I wrote about hearing God in silence, it was because most of us are surrounded by so much noise that we forget God often speaks softly. Psalm 46:10 says,

"Be still, and know that I am God." Stillness is where recognition begins.

Mark 1:35 shows Jesus modeling that.

"Very early in the morning, while it was still dark, Jesus got up, left the house and went off to a solitary place, where He prayed."

And Isaiah 30:15 reminds us,

"In repentance and rest is your salvation, in quietness and trust is your strength."

You don't have to fill the silence. You just have to enter it.

Finding God in the Everyday

Faith doesn't live only in sacred moments. God meets you in ordinary ones too. Paul wrote,

"So whether you eat or drink or whatever you do, do it all for the glory of God." *(1 Corinthians 10:31)* That's permission to bring God into everything you do.

Colossians 3:23 adds,

"Whatever you do, work at it with all your heart, as working for the Lord, not for human masters."

And Proverbs 3:6 ties it all together.

"In all your ways acknowledge Him, and He will make your paths straight."

God doesn't hide in church walls. He walks with you through grocery aisles, traffic lights, and Tuesday mornings.

Turning the Other Cheek

When I wrote that turning the other cheek doesn't mean being soft or letting people walk all over you, I wanted to show that Jesus wasn't teaching weakness. He was teaching strength under control. He said,

"If anyone slaps you on the right cheek, turn to them the other also." *(Matthew 5:38–39)*

That wasn't an invitation to be a doormat. It was a challenge to stay rooted in peace when the world expects retaliation.

Paul echoed this in Romans 12.

"Do not repay anyone evil for evil. Be careful to do what is right in the eyes of everyone... Do not be overcome by evil, but overcome evil with good." *(Romans 12:17–21)*

And Proverbs 15:1 reminds us,

"A gentle answer turns away wrath, but a harsh word stirs up anger."

It takes more strength to stay calm than to strike back. Turning the other cheek doesn't mean you agree with what was done. It means you refuse to let it define who you are.

Flipping Tables

When I talked about Jesus flipping tables, I wanted you to see that righteous anger isn't the same as outbursts or chaos. Jesus didn't lose control. He acted with purpose.

"Jesus entered the temple courts and drove out all who were buying and selling there. He overturned the tables of the money changers and the benches of those selling doves." *(Matthew 21:12–13)*

He wasn't throwing a tantrum. He was protecting what was holy.

Ephesians 4:26 gives us the right framework.

"In your anger do not sin. Do not let the sun go down while you are still angry."

And Isaiah 1:17 tells us,

"Learn to do right. Seek justice. Defend the oppressed."

There's a time to turn the other cheek, and there's a time to turn over tables. The key is knowing the difference.

Walking With Integrity

Integrity is doing what's right when nobody's watching. When I wrote about living in alignment between what you believe and how you behave, that came straight from Proverbs.

"Whoever walks in integrity walks securely, but whoever takes crooked paths will be found out." *(Proverbs 10:9)*

Integrity isn't perfection. It's consistency.

Psalm 15 describes the kind of person who lives that way.

"The one whose walk is blameless, who does what is righteous, who speaks the truth from their heart." *(Psalm 15:1–2)*

James reinforces that same message.

"Do not merely listen to the word and so deceive yourselves. Do what it says." *(James 1:22)*

Integrity isn't about image. It's about peace.

Forgiveness and Freedom

When I wrote that forgiveness doesn't mean what happened was okay, I wanted you to know that forgiveness is freedom, not approval. Jesus made forgiveness non-negotiable for a reason.

"For if you forgive other people when they sin against you, your heavenly Father will also forgive you." *(Matthew 6:14–15)*

Paul said it this way.

"Be kind and compassionate to one another, forgiving each other, just as in Christ God forgave you." *(Ephesians 4:31–32)*

And Colossians 3:13 adds,

"Bear with each other and forgive one another if any of you has a grievance against someone. Forgive as the Lord forgave you."

You don't forgive because they deserve it. You forgive because you deserve peace.

Serving Others With Purpose

When I said that serving is an act of worship, not an obligation, that came from the way Jesus lived.

"For even the Son of Man did not come to be served, but to serve, and to give His life as a ransom for many." *(Mark 10:45)*

Serving isn't about being seen. It's about love in action. Paul wrote,

"You, my brothers and sisters, were called to be free. But do not use your freedom to indulge the flesh. Rather, serve one another humbly in love." *(Galatians 5:13)*

And Philippians 2 reminds us to lead with humility.

"Do nothing out of selfish ambition or vain conceit. Rather, in humility value others above yourselves." *(Philippians 2:3–4)*

When you serve others, you're never lowering yourself. You're stepping into the same posture Jesus took.

Faith in the Storm

When I talked about trusting God when everything feels out of control, that came from moments just like the ones the disciples faced on the water.

"A furious squall came up, and the waves broke over the boat. Jesus was in the stern, sleeping on a cushion... He got up, rebuked the wind and said to the waves, 'Quiet! Be still!'" *(Mark 4:35–41)*

Faith isn't proven in calm seas. It's proven in storms.

James wrote,

"Consider it pure joy, my brothers and sisters, whenever you face trials of many kinds, because you know that the testing of your faith produces perseverance." *(James 1:2–4)*

And Isaiah 43:2 promises,

"When you pass through the waters, I will be with you."

The storm doesn't mean God forgot you. It means He's about to show you who He really is.

When Bad Things Happen

When I wrote about darkness being the absence of light, I wanted to help you see that evil and pain aren't equal to God. They're what happens when His presence, His love, or His order are rejected. The Bible says it clearly.

"God is light; in him there is no darkness at all." *1 John 1:5*

That verse isn't just about morality. It's about reality. Everything that is good, pure, and whole comes from Him. When creation turned away from that light, the world fell into shadow. That's what sin did. It fractured what God made perfect.

Even in Genesis, the first thing God created was light. He spoke into the chaos and said, "Let there be light." Darkness didn't stand a chance.

"And God said, 'Let there be light,' and there was light. God saw that the light was good, and he separated the light from the darkness." *Genesis 1:3–4*

That same truth still stands today. Wherever His light shows up, darkness loses.

I also mentioned that Jesus didn't avoid pain. He entered it. He told His disciples,

"In this world you will have trouble. But take heart! I have overcome the world." *John 16:33*

That promise doesn't mean life will be easy. It means that pain doesn't get the last word. Jesus has already defeated the darkness that tries to consume us.

Paul echoed that in Romans when he wrote,

"And we know that in all things God works for the good of those who love him, who have been called according to his purpose." *Romans 8:28*

That verse doesn't claim that all things are good. It promises that nothing is beyond redemption.

And even in suffering, the Psalms remind us that God isn't far away.

"The Lord is close to the brokenhearted and saves those who are crushed in spirit." *Psalm 34:18*

That's who He is. Not a distant observer but a present healer.

So when bad things happen, it's okay to question. It's okay to grieve. But don't mistake the darkness for God's absence. Darkness can't exist where light remains.

And the light still shines.

"The light shines in the darkness, and the darkness has not overcome it." *John 1:5*

That's the promise that holds when everything else falls apart.

The Quiet Season

When I wrote about God's silence, I wanted to remind you that it's not new. Every person who's ever walked closely with Him has faced a season where His voice felt far away. David, who was called a man after God's own heart, felt it deeply.

"Why, Lord, do you stand far off? Why do you hide yourself in times of trouble?" *Psalm 10:1*

He went from singing joyfully to crying out in confusion, but even in his questions, he never stopped talking to God. That's what real faith looks like — honesty in the silence.

Jesus experienced that same feeling on the cross. In His greatest pain, He echoed David's own words.

"My God, my God, why have you forsaken me?" *Matthew 27:46*

If the Son of God could feel distance and still choose trust, then our silence doesn't mean separation. It means we're being invited into deeper faith.

I mentioned Exodus 14:14 because it captures the quiet season perfectly. God told His people to stop striving and simply stand still.

"The Lord will fight for you; you need only to be still." *Exodus 14:14*

And Psalm 46:10 says the same truth another way.

"Be still, and know that I am God." *Psalm 46:10*

Stillness isn't about inactivity. It's about trust — choosing to believe that God is still moving even when you can't see it yet.

This season is where roots grow deep. The Bible shows again and again that silence comes before strength. Elijah didn't hear God in the wind or the fire, but in the gentle whisper.

"After the fire came a gentle whisper." *1 Kings 19:12*

If it feels like heaven's gone quiet, it hasn't. God is still near. Sometimes the silence is how He teaches us to recognize His voice again when He speaks.

That's the lesson of the quiet season: God isn't gone. He's growing you.

Finding Your Faith Family

When I wrote about finding a community that fits your walk, I meant the kind of connection the early church had.

"They devoted themselves to the apostles' teaching and to fellowship, to the breaking of bread and to prayer." *(Acts 2:42–47)*

Faith was never meant to be walked alone. Hebrews 10:24-25 says,

"Let us consider how we may spur one another on toward love and good deeds, not giving up meeting together."

And Paul described it this way,

"For just as each of us has one body with many members, and these members do not all have the same function, so in Christ we, though many, form one body." *(Romans 12:4–5)*

The right faith family won't just make you feel welcome. They'll make you grow.

Spiritual Mentors and Accountability

When I said you need people who tell you the truth with love, that wasn't just advice. It's a biblical principle.

"As iron sharpens iron, so one person sharpens another." *(Proverbs 27:17)*

Proverbs 11:14 adds,

"Where there is no guidance, a people falls, but in an abundance of counselors there is safety."

And Paul wrote to the Galatians,

"If someone is caught in a sin, you who live by the Spirit should restore that person gently. But watch yourselves, or you also may be tempted." *(Galatians 6:1–2)*

Accountability isn't control. It's protection. The right mentor doesn't just cheer for you. They guard your growth.

Faith for Sale

When I wrote about faith being used as a business model instead of a calling, I wanted to remind you that Jesus confronted that exact problem. He walked into the temple and saw people turning worship into profit.

"Jesus entered the temple courts and drove out all who were buying and selling there. He overturned the tables of the money changers and the benches of those selling doves." *(Matthew 21:12–13)*

The issue wasn't money. It was motive. Paul warned Timothy about that same temptation.

"Some think that godliness is a means to financial gain. But godliness with contentment is great gain." *(1 Timothy 6:5–6)*

And Peter spoke directly to false teachers who exploit faith for personal advantage.

"In their greed these teachers will exploit you with fabricated stories. Their condemnation has long been hanging over them." *(2 Peter 2:3)*

The point isn't to judge others. It's to stay alert to the fruit. When faith starts building fences instead of bigger tables, something's gone wrong.

Holy Excuses

When I wrote about people using faith as a shield instead of a mirror, that came from what Jesus warned about more than once. He saw people use religion to look holy on the outside while ignoring what needed healing inside. In Matthew 23, He called out the Pharisees for cleaning the outside of the cup while the inside was still dirty. It's a reminder that image can't replace integrity.

"Woe to you, teachers of the law and Pharisees, you hypocrites! You clean the outside of the cup and dish, but inside they are full of greed and self-indulgence." *Matthew 23:25–26*

When I said you can almost always find a verse to justify anything if you want to, I was thinking of how even the enemy used Scripture to tempt Jesus. That moment shows how dangerous it is to use the Word to serve our own will instead of submitting to God's.

"The devil took Him to the holy city and had Him stand on the highest point of the temple. 'If you are the Son of God,' he said, 'throw yourself down. For it is written...'" *Matthew 4:5–7*

Paul warned about the same trap when he said grace isn't permission to keep living the same way. God's mercy isn't a loophole. It's an invitation to change.

"What shall we say, then? Shall we go on sinning so that grace may increase? By no means! We are those who have died to sin; how can we live in it any longer?" *Romans 6:1–2*

I also mentioned that correction is part of walking with God. Proverbs says it bluntly, because truth isn't meant to flatter us. It's meant to free us.

"Whoever loves discipline loves knowledge, but whoever hates correction is stupid." *Proverbs 12:1*

And when Jesus said not everyone who calls Him "Lord" will enter the kingdom, He was making it clear that faith isn't about titles or talk. It's about obedience.

"Not everyone who says to me, 'Lord, Lord,' will enter the kingdom of heaven, but only the one who does the will of my Father who is in heaven." *Matthew 7:21*

This chapter was written as a reminder that twisting Scripture to avoid growth isn't faith — it's fear in disguise. Real faith doesn't use God as a shield from accountability. It lets His Word transform how we live, even when it's uncomfortable.

Iron Sharpens Iron

When I talked about people who make you better, not just people who make you comfortable, I was describing the kind of friendships Scripture tells us to build.

"As iron sharpens iron, so one person sharpens another." *(Proverbs 27:17)*

Real accountability creates growth, not guilt. Ecclesiastes 4:9-10 says,

"Two are better than one, because they have a good return for their labor. If either of them falls down, one can help the other up."

And Paul encouraged believers to teach each other with wisdom.

"Let the message of Christ dwell among you richly as you teach and admonish one another with all wisdom." *(Colossians 3:16)*

Sharpening sometimes creates friction, but that's how strength is formed.

Faith at Home

When I wrote that faith starts where you live, it came from a simple truth. The most honest version of your faith is the one your family sees. Joshua declared it clearly.

"But as for me and my household, we will serve the Lord." *(Joshua 24:15)*

Moses told the people of Israel to pass their faith to their children through conversation and example.

"These commandments that I give you today are to be on your hearts. Impress them on your children. Talk about them when you sit at home and when you walk along the road." *(Deuteronomy 6:6–7)*

And Paul reminded families that love and leadership work hand in hand.

"Husbands, love your wives, just as Christ loved the church and gave himself up for her." *(Ephesians 5:25)*

Faith at home isn't about preaching. It's about practicing.

Faith at Work

When I said that faith at work isn't about being loud, it's about being consistent, I meant exactly what Paul taught.

"Whatever you do, work at it with all your heart, as working for the Lord, not for human masters." *(Colossians 3:23–24)*

Jesus told His followers,

"Let your light shine before others, that they may see your good deeds and glorify your Father in heaven." *(Matthew 5:16)*

And Peter encouraged believers to live in a way that earns respect even among those who don't share their faith.

"Live such good lives among the pagans that, though they accuse you of doing wrong, they may see your good deeds and glorify God." *(1 Peter 2:12)*

Faith doesn't need a pulpit to speak. It just needs consistency.

Sharing Your Faith Authentically

When I said that sharing your faith isn't about arguing or convincing, I was thinking of Peter's advice.

"Always be prepared to give an answer to everyone who asks you to give the reason for the hope that you have. But do this with gentleness and respect." *(1 Peter 3:15)*

Jesus said that your life itself is proof of His work.

"You are the light of the world. A city built on a hill cannot be hidden." *(Matthew 5:14–16)*

And He added another clue about how people will recognize His followers.

"By this everyone will know that you are my disciples, if you love one another." *(John 13:35)*

You don't have to talk louder. You just have to love better.

Discipleship in Real Life

When I wrote that discipleship is about walking with people, not controlling them, I was echoing Jesus' final words to His followers.

"Therefore go and make disciples of all nations, baptizing them in the name of the Father and of the Son and of the Holy Spirit, and teaching them to obey everything I have commanded you." *(Matthew 28:19–20)*

Paul told Timothy to keep the cycle going.

"The things you have heard me say in the presence of many witnesses entrust to reliable people who will also be qualified to teach others." *(2 Timothy 2:2)*

And Jesus modeled it best when He said,

"I have set you an example that you should do as I have done for you." *(John 13:15)*

Discipleship is less about titles and more about time. You grow by walking together.

Purpose and Calling

When I wrote that purpose isn't something you chase but something you uncover, I meant that God's plan for you already exists.

"And we know that in all things God works for the good of those who love Him, who have been called according to His purpose." *(Romans 8:28)*

Paul reminded the church in Ephesus,

"For we are God's handiwork, created in Christ Jesus to do good works, which God prepared in advance for us to do." *(Ephesians 2:10)*

And Proverbs 19:21 puts it plainly.

"Many are the plans in a person's heart, but it is the Lord's purpose that prevails."

Purpose isn't about position. It's about obedience.

Letting Your Light Shine

When I said your life doesn't need a spotlight to shine, that came straight from Jesus' teaching.

"You are the light of the world. A city on a hill cannot be hidden." *(Matthew 5:14–16)*

Paul wrote to the Philippians,

"Do everything without grumbling or arguing, so that you may become blameless and pure, children of God without fault in a warped and crooked generation. Then you will shine among them like stars in the sky." *(Philippians 2:15)*

And Peter said,

"You are a chosen people, a royal priesthood, a holy nation, God's special possession, that you may declare the praises of Him who called you out of darkness into His wonderful light." *(1 Peter 2:9)*

Your light doesn't compete with anyone else's. It simply points to the source.

Legacy of Faith

When I wrote that legacy isn't about what you leave behind but who you leave behind, I wanted to remind you that faith multiplies through people. Paul finished his race with confidence, saying,

"I have fought the good fight, I have finished the race, I have kept the faith." *(2 Timothy 4:7)*

Moses told the people of Israel to make their faith generational.

"Love the Lord your God with all your heart and with all your soul and with all your strength. Impress these commandments on your children." *(Deuteronomy 6:5–9)*

And Paul encouraged the church,

"Let us not become weary in doing good, for at the proper time we will reap a harvest if we do not give up." *(Galatians 6:9)*

Legacy isn't built in moments. It's built in faithfulness.

The Daily Decision

When I said faith isn't something you master but something you practice, that came from Jesus' own invitation.

"Whoever wants to be my disciple must deny themselves and take up their cross daily and follow me." *(Luke 9:23)*

Paul echoed the same mindset.

"I press on toward the goal to win the prize for which God has called me heavenward in Christ Jesus." *(Philippians 3:14)*

And Hebrews reminds us to stay focused on the long view.

"Let us run with endurance the race that is set before us, fixing our eyes on Jesus, the pioneer and perfecter of faith." *(Hebrews 12:1–2)*

Faith grows in repetition. Every day you choose to show up again, you strengthen what matters most.

Final Note

Every truth in this book traces back to these verses. They're not just references. They're reminders that everything I've shared is already written in the Word.

If something here encouraged you, go back and read the full passages for yourself. Sit with them. Pray through them. Let them speak to you personally. That's how faith grows — not by memorizing what's written, but by letting it move from your head to your heart.

This whole journey of showing up more spiritually is really about learning to hear God for yourself. These Scriptures are the doorway to that. Keep walking through it. Keep learning. Keep listening.

Because the more time you spend in His Word, the more clearly you'll recognize His voice in your world.

That's how you build a faith that lasts.

9 798998 893872